D0413781

EDMUND CAMPION

An imaginary portrait by Reynolds Stone
based on contemporary records and pictures of the martyr
made shortly after his death

EVELYN WAUGH

EDMUND
CAMPION

Oxford New York Toronto Melbourne
OXFORD UNIVERSITY PRESS
1980

Oxford University Press, Walton Street, Oxford OX2 6DP

OXFORD LONDON GLASGOW
NEW YORK TORONTO MELBOURNE WELLINGTON
KUALA LUMPUR SINGAPORE JAKARTA HONG KONG TOKYO
DELHI BOMBAY CALCUTTA MADRAS KARACHI
NAIROBI DAR ES SALAAM CAPE TOWN

© Campion Hall 1980

First published 1935
Third edition 1961
First published as an Oxford University Press paperback 1980

British Library Cataloguing in Publication Data
Waugh, Evelyn
Edmund Campion — 3rd ed.
1. Campion, Edmund, Saint
2. Christian saints — England — Biography
3. Jesuits — England — Biography
271'.53'024 BX4705.C27 79–41285
ISBN 0–19–281287–4

Printed in Great Britain by
Cox & Wyman Ltd, Reading

To
M. C. D'ARCY, S.J.
Sometime Master of Campion Hall
Oxford

CONTENTS

PREFACE

In 1934, when Campion Hall, Oxford, was being rebuilt on a site and in a manner more worthy of its distinction than its old home in St. Giles's, I wished to do something to mark my joy in the occasion and my gratitude to the then Master, to whom, under God, I owe my faith. A life of the Blessed Edmund Campion seemed the most suitable memorial. The alternatives were either a drastic revision of Richard Simpson's excellent work, which had long been out of print and had been corrected in many particulars by subsequent research, or to attempt an entirely new book. I chose the latter but Simpson's strong foundations support my structure and it is to him that I owe the greatest debt. I received invaluable help from Father Basset and Father Booth, from the late Father Watts of Stonyhurst, Father Hicks of Farm Street and Mr. Douglas Woodruff. I was privileged to use the copious collection of notes and documents collected by one of the Fathers at Farm Street for what would have been, had he lived, the definitive biography.

There is great need for a complete, scholar's work on the subject. This is not it. All I have done is select the incidents which struck a novelist as important, and relate them in a single narrative.

It shall be read as a simple, perfectly true story of heroism and holiness.

We have come much nearer to Campion since Simpson's

day. He wrote in the flood-tide of toleration when Elizabeth's persecution seemed as remote as Diocletian's. We know now that his age was a brief truce in an unending war. The Martyrdom of Father Pro in Mexico re-enacted Campion's in faithful detail. We are nearer Campion than when I wrote of him. We have seen the Church drawn underground in country after country. In fragments and whispers we get news of other saints in the prison camps of Eastern and South-eastern Europe, of cruelty and degradation more savage than anything in Tudor England, of the same, pure light shining in darkness, uncomprehended. The haunted, trapped, murdered priest is our contemporary and Campion's voice sounds to us across the centuries as though he were walking at our elbow.

EVELYN WAUGH

PART I

THE SCHOLAR

THE SCHOLAR

In the middle of March 1603 it was clear to everyone that Queen Elizabeth was dying; her doctors were unable to diagnose the illness; she had little fever, but was constantly thirsty, restless and morose; she refused to take medicine, refused to eat, refused to go to bed. She sat on the floor, propped up with cushions, sleepless and silent, her eyes constantly open, fixed on the ground, oblivious to the coming and going of her councillors and attendants. She had done nothing to recognize her successor; she had made no provision for the disposal of her personal property, of the vast, heterogeneous accumulation of a lifetime, in which presents had come to her daily from all parts of the world; closets and cupboards stacked high with jewellery, coin, bric-à-brac; the wardrobe of two thousand outmoded dresses. There was always company in the little withdrawing room waiting for her to speak, but she sighed and sipped and kept her silence. She had round her neck a piece of gold the size of an angel, engraved with characters; it had been left to her lately by a wise woman who had died in Wales at the age of a hundred and twenty. Sir John Stanhope had assured her that as long as she wore this talisman she could not die. There was no need yet for doctors or lawyers or statesmen or clergy.

Lord Admiral Howard was one of her visitors. He knelt beside her and, with tears, implored her to take a little nourishment. They brought a bowl of broth and the Admiral coaxed her to take a spoonful or two from his own hands. But when he urged her to go to bed she refused angrily, breaking into a confused and violent tale of her nightmares.

'If you were in the habit of seeing such things in your bed, as I do in mine,' she said, 'you would not persuade me to go there.'

But she had not the strength to sustain her rage, and, when Cecil and the lawyers had left her, she shook her head piteously, saying, 'My lord, I am tied with a chain of iron about my neck.'

The Admiral reminded her of her wonted courage, but she replied, desponding, 'I am tied, I am tied; and the case is altered with me.'

The Council sent the Archbishop of Canterbury to her; he came with several other divines, eloquent, circumspect men who had made a great career in her Church, to offer the consolations of religion; but their appearance roused her to fury. She rated them and sent them packing, crying that she was no atheist, but she knew full well they were but hedge priests.

The women about her tried to attribute causes to her melancholy; it was due to the execution of Essex, the execution of Mary of Scotland, the pardon of Tyrone. She herself confided to Lady Scrope that, before the Court moved from Whitehall, she had seen a hideous vision of 'her own body, exceeding lean and fearful in a light of fire'. She had asked, too, for a 'true looking-glass', which she had not seen for twenty years, and when it was brought fell exclaiming at all the flatterers that had so much commended her.

All her life she had been surrounded by plots; plots to implicate her in Wyatt's rebellion, plots against her life, to murder her with fire balls, to poison the pommel of her saddle; many of them real enough, some fomented by *agents provocateurs,* some the inventions of forgers and informers, plots that had no existence except in the brains of Walsingham and the Cecils. Now in her last illness they took shape again, and assassins lurked for her in the darkness and behind the curtains.

So she lay for nearly two weeks, until, lapsing into a stupor, she was carried to bed, where she died without speaking. The Archbishop returned to her at the end, and a movement of the hand was interpreted by her ladies-in-waiting as her consent to his presence.

In these circumstances the Tudor dynasty came to an end, which in three generations had changed the aspect and temper of England. They left a new aristocracy, a new religion, a new system of government; the generation was already in its childhood that was to send King Charles to the scaffold; the new, rich families who were to introduce the House of Hanover were already in the second stage of their metamorphosis from the freebooters of Edward VI's reign to the conspirators of 1688 and the sceptical, cultured oligarchs of the eighteenth century. The vast exuberance of the Renaissance had been canalized. England was secure, independent, insular; the course of her history lay plain ahead; competitive nationalism, competitive industrialism, competitive imperialism, the looms and coal mines and counting houses, the joint-stock companies and the cantonments; the power and the weakness of great possessions.

What was in Elizabeth's mind as she lay there through the silent hours, sane and despairing? The thought of another England that it had been in her hands to make? Or did she contrast her present state, an old perjured woman, dying without comfort, with those early years when the future had been compact of hope and adventure; see the light on the river and hear again the splash of oars as Leicester's barge rode between green banks and pollarded willows, and the flowered damask trailed out in the water behind them; the torchlight at Kenilworth and Rycote, the extravagant, irresponsible dances before the royal suitors, the bonfires kindling from crest to crest as the news travelled across country of the Armada's failure? . . . It had been a life of tumultuous drama, and it was ending, now, in silence; among all its incidents did she recall the afternoon of high summer when she had moved in a great retinue from Woodstock to Oxford, and, for the first time, held her Court among the scholars of the University?

The visit had been twice postponed. Two years earlier— in 1564—she had been to Cambridge, where the whole University had exerted itself in her entertainment, some of the more enthusiastic members even following her on the first stage of the return journey and attempting to make themselves agreeable to her—unsuccessfully, as things turned out—by performing a burlesque of the Mass, in which one of them, dressed as a dog, capered about the stage with a Host in his mouth. She had meant to proceed to Oxford at that time, but the plague, brought over by the defeated garrison from Dieppe, still hung about the city, and it was not until the summer of 1566 that it was thought safe for the eagerly expected visit to take place.

Although it was vacation time, practically the whole University remained in residence for her coming. The Court was at the Palace of Woodstock, a short journey away, and at the end of August, on an afternoon of heavy rain, Leicester, who was now Chancellor of the University, Sir William Cecil and a few companions rode over to make the final arrangements. Two days later—Saturday, 31st—the Queen followed them, attended by most of the Court and the Spanish Ambassador. Leicester came to meet her at Wolvercote, the boundary of the University Liberties; with him were the Vice-Chancellor and the Heads of Houses in their academic robes.

It was a formidable afternoon. From the moment that the gay and chattering procession crossed into university ground, the character of their reception became manifest. That day, at any rate, there was to be no levity; nor was there to be any haste. The cavalcade halted while the Provost of Oriel pronounced in laboriously polished Latin an address of welcome, which can have been intelligible to very few of the attendant ladies and gentlemen—the Earl of Warwick, Leicester's brother, a tough, middle-aged soldier; Edward de Vere, Earl of Oxford, aged sixteen, Cecil's son-in-law, but a child of the old nobility, soon to get into trouble for murdering a servant; young Edward Manners, Duke of Rutland—all sitting patiently on their horses while the phrases of the oration rose and fell in the best Ciceronian style. At length it came to an end, compliments were exchanged, and the procession moved off. A few miles farther

on another little cluster of notables was assembled—the
Mayor of the City and the civic dignitaries. Here the
speeches were in English, but at the North Gate another don
was in wait for them, Mr. Deal of New College, with an
oration in Latin. From the gate to Carfax the way was lined
with kneeling and applauding scholars; this was the kind of
thing to which the Court was accustomed, but at Carfax
came another check, Lawrence the Regius Professor, with a
composition in Greek. It was the finest oration, the Queen
said, that she had ever heard in Greek; she was prepared for
an exchange of pleasantries in the same language, but, in
pity for the evident distress of her followers, she consented
to postpone it until they reached their lodgings. The company moved on again, litter and hackney, but the speeches
were not yet over. At the gates of Christ Church Mr.
Kingsmill, the University Orator, was ready to welcome
them. The Queen heard him to the end, but, grown slightly
testy by this time, merely remarked in acknowledgment,
'You would have done well had you had good matter.'

The Court crossed the threshold of the House; they were
now among the very buildings where most of them were
to be quartered, but their hosts had not yet done with them.
Four Doctors in their scarlet robes were observed advancing
upon the royal party across the quadrangle, carrying a
canopy; under this Elizabeth was led to church where, in
sonorous English, prayers were offered in thanksgiving for
her safe arrival; an anthem was sung to the music of cornets;
after the anthem there were more prayers. At last, late in the
evening, the weary courtiers were allowed to disperse, to
see to their baggage and their beds, to wash and refresh

themselves, while the young Queen stole away to her lodgings through the gathering shadows of Dr. Westphaling's garden.

The visit lasted for six days. There were some lighter moments: a Latin play in Christ Church Hall, called *Marcus Geminus,* which the Queen did not attend (the Spanish Ambassador spoke so highly of it that she resolved to lose no more sport thereafter); an English play acted in two parts named *Palamon and Arcite,* at the first night of which the stage collapsed, killing three people and injuring five more; on the second night a pack of hounds was introduced into the quadrangle, which moved the young scholars, confined to the upper storeys, to such excitement that the Queen expressed her fear that they would fall out of the windows; there were several elaborate dinners; but for the most part the entertainment was strictly academic; orations, sermons, debates, the presentation of Latin verses translated from the Hebrew, the conferring of honorary degrees.

It was not until the third day, Tuesday, September 3rd, when the senior members had played their parts, that Edmund Campion made his appearance. He was then twenty-six years old, seven years younger than the Queen, but already a person of outstanding importance in the University. At the age of seventeen he had become a Fellow of St. John's, and almost immediately attracted round him a group of pupils over whom he exerted an effortless and comprehensive influence; they crowded to his lectures, imitated his habits of speech, his mannerisms and his clothes, and were proud to style themselves 'Campionists'. There had been a certain difficulty in choosing suitable subjects for debate, for the subject in everyone's mind at Oxford and on everyone's tongue was the Queen's change of religion; Cecil had carefully edited the list of propositions, eliminating Jewel's attempt to bring matters to an issue; it was well known that Oxford, and particularly St. John's, was predominantly Catholic in sympathy; the last thing that he wanted was to embarrass the occasion by arousing the theological passions that had flamed into disorder when Peter Martyr had been Professor of Divinity. Discussion was confined to strictly secular subjects, and to Campion fell the task of proposing 'that the tides are caused by the moon's motion', and 'that the lower bodies of the universe are regulated by the higher'.

Throughout his career Campion preserved a naïve interest in natural science, and later, in the dark hours when he was fighting for his reputation in Hopton's Hall, he was willing to prove to his judges that the heavens were as hard as crystal. Now he seems to have treated the question at issue as a subordinate matter; all his eloquence, the delicate accent, the terse, stylish antitheses, the strong and accurate diction, that made him the model of the schools, was devoted to the praise of the Queen and the Vice-Chancellor. Speaking in Latin, he began: 'One thing only reconciles me to the unequal contest, which I must maintain single-handed against four pugnacious youths; that I am speaking in the name of Philosophy, the princess of letters, before Elizabeth, the lettered princess.'

He praised the learning of her ancestors and her condescension in visiting her poor scholars; then he turned to the Earl of Leicester, who sat beside her, and reminded him that it was due to his godly and deathless benefactions that the University had thrown off its lethargy and was once more advancing in hope.

'May God preserve these benefits to us; may He preserve,' bowing left and right, 'your Majesty, your Honour; you our mother, you our protector—*te quae haec facis, te qui haec mones'*, at which the Queen, turning smiling in her seat towards the Earl said: 'You, my lord, must still be one.'

The balanced compliments succeeded one another, until, remarking that the poor scholars had no fit present to offer their visitors except what was within them, something from 'the veins and bowels of philosophy', Campion proceeded to his subject and briefly expounded the theory that the sea was constantly blown out with vapours, like water boiling in a pot.

The speech was the success of the afternoon. The Queen warmly applauded and commended Campion to Leicester, and later, when the Spanish Ambassador remarked that, though laudable, the speeches were, after all, well prepared beforehand, and the Queen assembled the most notable orators for an extempore debate at Merton, Campion was among them, and spoke on the subject of 'Fire' in a way to confirm her highest opinions of him. Before leaving Oxford, both Cecil and Leicester saw Campion privately, and promised him their patronage.

He could hardly have been offered two more different patrons—the secretary, purposeful, cautious, self-controlled, indefatigable, middle-class, the man of the desk and the Council table; and the flamboyant courtier, swarthy and swaggering, magnificent, impulsive, a spectacular horseman, a soldier; descended on one side from the great families of English history, Talbot and Beauchamp, on the other from the reckless, bloodstained house of Dudley; three generations of Dudleys, his grandfather, his father and his brother, had died on the scaffold; perhaps no one in Oxford doubted that Amy Robsart, whose obsequies four years before they had piously celebrated, had been murdered at his orders. At any hour he might become the Queen's husband. His was all the glamour of the great world that lay beyond the University Liberties; the pageantry and the high politics of the new reign. It was to him that Campion immediately attached himself.

And Leicester did not neglect his satellite. At Woodstock and Rycote, when the Court felt the need for a serious interlude, it was often Campion who was summoned to minister to them. For, though to the dazzled young scholar their world might seem something intangibly remote, those in power knew very well that they had need of men like Campion. There had been a grave purpose behind the visit to Oxford.

For the past twenty-five years education in England had been in a state of disorder which threatened at any moment to become chaos. At the beginning of the century Erasmus had placed English scholarship above that of France or the Germanies, second only to Italy in its breadth of culture. It was to England that the University of Leipsic had turned for its professor of Greek; Colet, Grocyn, Linacre and More were able to converse on terms of equality with the leading men of Padua, and under their temperate and profound influence Oxford was emerging gradually, steadily, by a

process of organic growth, from the cloistered formality of
the Middle Ages into the spacious, luminous world of
Catholic humanism. With the Pope's encouragement
Wolsey had taken over monastic revenues for the endow-
ment of Christ Church; Fox, Bishop of Winchester, insti-
tuted the first Greek lectureship in the foundation of Corpus;
the faction of 'Trojans' who were opposed to the new learning were being gently pressed into acquiescence by the King
and the Bishops. Close correspondence was kept with the
great teachers of Italy, and the foundations were laid of a
Renaissance which, illuminated by the poetic genius native
to the country, might, in a generation, have been one of the
glories of Europe.

All this ended abruptly and violently at Henry's break
with the Pope. When the Church was in undisputed authority she could afford to wink at a little speculative fancy in her
philosophers, a pagan exuberance of taste in her artists; now,
when she was driven to defend the basis and essential structure of her faith, there was no room for indulgence; controversy took first place among the Arts, and scholars
became famous for their views on the Mass rather than their
appreciation of classical poetry.

More than this, the confiscators of ecclesiastical property
made havoc of university finance. Education all over the
country was dependent upon monastic and chantry foundations, and at their suppression grammar-school education in
many districts came utterly to an end. Here and there the
revenues of the dispossessed religious were kept for public
services, and a few reorganized grammar schools survived
under charters of Edward VI, but in the great majority of

cases the estates went direct to the courtiers. At Oxford the
Colleges were a comparatively new institution, and a large
part of university life still centred in the halls which the
various abbeys and priories maintained for their students.
These were all emptied; the undergraduates dependent on
monastic exhibitions were turned adrift and the Colleges
themselves entertained well-founded apprehensions of how
long they would be allowed to survive. The courtiers both
of Henry VIII and of Somerset had pressed for their abolition;
the demand, in both cases, was resisted and rebuked, but
the thirst for plunder was not slaked and it is possible that,
if Edward VI had lived some years longer, both universities
would have come to grief. As it was, the visitors of Edward
VI suppressed many of the exhibitions for poor students
which had survived the acts of confiscation, and only the
strenuous protests of the citizens saved Magdalen Grammar
School from extinction. The college chapels were ransacked
of Popish ornaments; the great reredos of All Souls was
destroyed, and New College windows only survived on the
Fellows' promise to have them out, as soon as they could
afford to replace them with plain glass; but it was upon
books that the Anglicans particularly turned their dis-
approval. The whole of the Duke Humphrey's library was
gutted and the shelves sold in the streets; the illuminated
office books in Magdalen choir were hacked up with
choppers, and from every college cartloads of books were
removed to be burned or sold as waste paper; a coloured
initial was enough to convict the contents of Popery; a
mathematical diagram of magic. When the visitors left, the
collections of centuries had been irretrievably ruined.

Better order was restored under Mary. Two new colleges, St. John's and Trinity, were founded, but the past could not be recalled. There was another upheaval at Elizabeth's succession, and numerous Catholics lost their chairs and fellowships; no one felt confidence in the rewards of scholarship. Politics and theology continued to sway University elections. A great tradition had been broken. Not for a hundred years was the University to know security, and it was to emerge from its troubles provincial, phlegmatic and exclusive; not for three hundred years was it to re-emerge as a centre of national life.

Elizabeth and Cecil were well aware of these conditions. They had a genuine and deep respect for learning, and one object of the visit had been to assure the scholars of royal favour. In this they were successful; the numbers taking degrees show a marked increase from this time. But there was another and more delicate mission.

From its earliest days the University had been primarily a place for the training of churchmen. By the statutes, Holy Orders were obligatory on aspirants for almost all the important offices. Sons of the aristocracy might keep term in the interests of culture, but the general assumption for the poor scholars was that they were qualifying as priests. Now Cecil and Elizabeth were finding it very hard to get suitable candidates for ministry in the new Church. By the first acts of the reign they had made the Mass illegal and issued a Prayer Book based on the two experimental books of Edward VI. This had been done against the unanimous vote of Convocation, and it was followed by the resignation or deprivation of a considerable number of the clergy. It is impossible, through the absence of many of the records, to estimate at all accurately the number of parish priests who gave up their cures and drifted into penury or other employment—probably about five hundred—but the names of most of the higher clergy have been preserved, and these include the entire episcopate, with the exception of Kitchen of Llandaff, fifteen heads of colleges, ten deans, twelve archdeacons and forty-seven prebendaries. The new Church was thus starting its history with a painful shortage of qualified leaders. Those who preferred to accept the change and make careers for themselves in the Establishment against which they had protested were not the most desirable of the old body; reluctant acquiescence was the best for which Cecil and Elizabeth could hope, except from one quarter where support was wholly unwelcome. They had no more taste for the extremists of their own party than they had for the Catholics. Elizabeth's personal inclinations were towards something mildly ceremonious in public worship; she kept a cross and candles in her chapel, she preferred her ministers to be celibate and suitably vested, she liked to think that her Church had retained something from the tradition of her ancestors. Had she been born in an age which offered no alternative, she would have conformed complacently enough, for, apart from a pronounced deficiency in faith, hope and charity, she had in many ways a naturally Catholic temperament; Cecil, though more austere in taste, already divined in the theocratic system of Geneva and the wild oratory of St. Andrews the spirit that was later to wreck the monarchy; neither had any use for the fanatical Puritans. They needed, to guide their Church through her difficult infancy, a new kind of cleric; sober, decently educated men, with a proper devotion to the Crown and the Council, men of common sense who could see where their advantage lay, men of high repute who could override the suggestion that religion had fallen to the management of knaves and eccentrics. Inevitably, it was to the younger members of the universities that they turned; Campion seemed a man eminently suitable to their purpose. His charm and attainments were easily apparent; he was sprung from just that stock of London tradespeople where the chief strength of Protestantism lay; he was completely without resources, and had his way to make in the world.

There was another young Oxford man who attracted their particular attention, a Fellow of Christ Church named Tobie Matthew. He was younger than Campion, barely twenty years old, and had had no part in the debates in the schools. It was not until Elizabeth's last day in Oxford that he was presented to her, when he made a farewell oration which attracted her so much that she nominated him her scholar. Cecil looked after him well; a splendid career lay before him. He became Canon of Christ Church four years later; in 1572, at the unusually early age of twenty-six, he was made President of St. John's, where he set himself to release the college from its obligation to receive poor scholars elected from the Merchant Taylors; four years later he was Dean of Christ Church, later Vice-Chancellor; from there he turned to the greater world, became successively Dean and Bishop of Durham, and, finally, Archbishop of York. He was a talkative little man, always eager to please, always ready with a neat parsonic witticism; the best of good fellows everywhere, except in his own family. When, on the Council of the North, he was most busy hunting down recusants, he was full of little jokes to beguile his colleagues. He was a great preacher. At first he kept no count of his sermons, but later, realizing their importance, he scored them punctually in a book; between his elevation to the Deanery of Durham and his death he preached 1,992 times. In James's reign he saw the trend of the times, and, alone among the bishops, voted in favour of conference with the lower House. He married admirably, a widow of stout Protestant principles and unique place in the new clerical caste, which had sprung naturally from the system of married clergy: Frances Barlow, widow of Matthew Parker, Junior; she was notable in her generation as having a bishop for her father, an archbishop for her father-in-law, an archbishop for her husband, and four bishops for her brothers. Tobie Matthew died full of honours in 1628. There, but for the Grace of God, went Edmund Campion.

The visitors departed and the University settled down to its normal routine. At St. John's work started early with a lecture in logic at half-past six; at nine there was a Greek lecture; rhetoric at one or two; there were also university lectures once or twice in the week on divinity, grammar, physics and metaphysics. Mathematics was left to vacations. In hall the college dined at three tables, the Fellows and masters at one, bachelors and third-year undergraduates at another, the choristers and students at a third; recreation was limited to the bow and arrow. At night the scholars slept in a single, large dormitory, two in a bed, until they were over sixteen years of age. The Fellows and tutors had their own rooms, which they shared with a scholar deputed to work for them. Every scholar was put under the particular supervision of a tutor, who directed his studies, saw that his hair was trimmed and his manners orderly, and, when necessary, corrected him with the birch. The founder of the college, Sir Thomas White, had lived until 1564, and up to his death he saw to it that the rules he had laid down were properly observed. He was a city magnate of modest education and simple piety; a childless old man who devoted the whole of his great wealth to benefactions. The last years of his life were quite overclouded by the change of religion; he collected the sacred vessels from the college chapel and stored them away in his own house for a happier day, and was obliged to stand by helpless while the authorities perverted the ends of his own foundation; he saw the poor scholars whom he had adopted and designed for the priesthood trained in a new way of thought and ordained with different rites, for a different purpose. He had set down in his statutes that the day was to begin with Mass, said in the Sarum use; at Elizabeth's accession it ceased, never to be restored; he saw three of his Presidents, Belsire, Elye, and Stork, deposed by the authorities for their faith. He died a comparatively poor man, out of favour at Court, out of temper with the times, and was buried according to Protestant rites; Campion speaking the funeral oration in terms which appear rather patronizing.

Perhaps in secret a Mass was said for him; it is impossible to say. There were still many priests in Oxford, and at this time the greater part of St. John's was Catholic in sympathy, but no record survives of any such act, and it seems probable that from the early days of Elizabeth until the counter-reformationary period, fifteen or twenty years later, Catholicism at Oxford was largely a matter of sentiment and loyalty to the old ways, rather than of active spiritual life. The best men, like William Allen, had left the University and the country. Those that remained honoured the Church in much the same way as the dons of the eighteenth century were to honour the House of Stuart. At Merton they enjoyed singing Popish hymns round the fire at night, as a later generation were to sing Jacobite songs. But the saying of Mass was a different matter. Whatever the sectional differences between the various Anglican groups, they were united in their resolve to stamp out this vital practice of the old religion.

They struck hard at all the ancient habits of spiritual life —the rosary, devotion to Our Lady and the Saints, pilgrimages, religious art, fasting, confession, penance and the great succession of traditional holidays—but the Mass was recognized as being both the distinguishing sign and main sustenance of their opponents. The objects specially connected with it, the vestments, plate and missals, were singled out for destruction; the altar stones were taken for paving and cheese presses; they ridiculed the Host in broadsheets and burlesques, called it by derisive nicknames, 'Round Robin', 'Jack in the Box' and 'Wormes Meat'. 'Massing priests' is the phrase constantly used in Cecil's correspondence to designate the Marian priests; the right to have Mass said in a private chapel was one of the main questions at issue in the negotiations for Elizabeth's marriage with her Catholic suitors; one of the terms suggested for peace with Mary Stuart was that she should 'abandon the Mass in Scotland and receive Common Prayer after the form of England'. It was one of the complaints against de Quadra that he had allowed strangers to hear Mass in the Embassy Chapel. Other instances of the kind can be quoted almost interminably; many will occur in the course of this narrative. On occasions the feeling found extravagant expression. In July 1581 the congregation in St. Peter's at Rome was startled by an infuriated Anglican tourist who attempted to snatch the Host from the priest's hand, while in November of the same year another Englishman upset the chalice and attempted to strangle the priest in S. Maria del Popolo.

Opinion differed on the significance of the 'Lord's Supper or Holy Communion' service which had been composed in its place; it was employed as an occasional service for communicants only; not as the central act of worship; the wording was devised so as to embrace, as far as possible, the conflicting theories of Luther, Calvin, Zwingli and Bucer, but it was explicit in its dissociation from the Catholic Mass. It was on this very point—not of the Papal supremacy —that the condemned heretics of Mary's reign went to the stake; men and women of noble resolution to whom the new Church looked back as martyrs, worthy of the same veneration which Catholics paid to Fisher and More, and the record of whose sufferings, in Foxe's highly inaccurate chronicle, was placed beside the Bible in the churches.

The law at this period (1559–70) was mild in comparison with what it subsequently became; the priest, for saying Mass in public or private, was liable at the first conviction to one year's sequestration from his benefice and six months' imprisonment; at the second, to deprivation and a year's imprisonment; at the third, to imprisonment for life. Anyone inducing him to offend in this way was fined a hundred marks in the first case, four hundred in the second, and in the third forfeited his entire property and was imprisoned for life. But there do not appear to have been any convictions under this Act at Oxford. Later, in 1577, when the penalties were far heavier and more rigorously imposed, a Mr. Etheridge was arrested for having Mass said in his house; there seems, too, at that time, to have been a regular chapel frequented by Catholics in the cellars under the Mitre Inn, but during the time that Campion was in residence submission on this point may have been complete; the ambiguous attitude of himself and his contemporaries is easily explicable on the assumption that throughout the whole of this period they were entirely deprived of the sacraments.

He probably had taken the Oath of Supremacy when he became B.A. in 1560; he must have put in a fairly regular appearance at the Protestant services in the college chapel; in 1568 he committed himself more gravely by accepting ordination as deacon at the hands of his friend Cheney, Bishop of Gloucester. But it seems clear that he took this step to avoid rather than to invite prominence in ecclesiastical affairs. In this confused and ill-documented decade, the Catholics, left without effective leadership, appear to have been dealing with the problem of conformity each in his own way. It was one which varied greatly in different parts of the country. Some refused the oath and went into exile;

some paid the penalties of the law. Some, who were popular
or locally powerful, avoided, year after year, taking the oath
at all; some took the oath and meant nothing by it. That
generation was inured to change; sooner or later the tide
would turn in their favour again; a Protestant coup, such as
was spoken of, to enthrone the Earl of Huntingdon might
inflame a national rising and restore the old religion; the
Queen might die and be succeeded by Mary Stuart; she
might marry a Catholic; she might declare for Catholicism
herself. In any case, things were not likely to last on their
present unreasonable basis. It was one thing for a Government to suppress dangerous innovations—that was natural
enough; but for the innovators to be in command, for them
to try to crush out by force historic Christianity—that was
contrary to all good sense; it was like living under the
Turks. At the worst there would soon be a truce, and both
parties would practise their religions without interference.
So they muddled along, waiting for better times to come.
In many places the priest would say Mass in his own house
for the Catholics before proceeding to read Morning Prayer
in the parish church; occasionally, it is said, he would even
bring consecrated wafers and communicate his Catholic
parishioners at the same time as he distributed to the Protestants the bread blessed according to the new rite.

At Oxford the division was more sharply defined; there
was a Catholic party in the majority, and a Protestant party
in the ascendant. Campion hesitated between the two,
reluctant to decide. What he wished was to be left in peace
to pursue his own studies, to discharge the duties which
soon fell on him as proctor and public orator, to do his best

for his pupils. But he was born into the wrong age for these gentle ambitions; he must be either much more, or much less. By the statutes of the college he was obliged, if he wished to make his career in the University, to proceed to the study of theology and the acceptance of Holy Orders. He put it off as long as he could, concentrating at first upon Aristotle and natural theology, where there was little to entangle him in the controversies of the day, but in 1567 he had, in the normal course, to proceed to the study of the Fathers. Here every sentence seemed to bear a topical allusion, and the deeper he penetrated into the minds of the Doctors, the farther he seemed from the Anglican Church which he was designed to enter. He fled and doubled from the conclusions of his reason; nothing but ill was promised for him by the way he was being drawn; he prayed fervently, he consulted those about him. Shrewd little Tobie Matthew was recognized as a specialist on the subject. Earnestly, man to man, Campion asked him how, with his deep knowledge of the Fathers, he could take the side he did.

'If I believed them as well as read them,' Matthew replied, 'you would have good reason to ask.'

It was no longer a question of theology, but of morals. Campion could not, like Cheney of Gloucester, affect to recognize in Cecil's Establishment the ancient Church of Augustine and Thomas à Becket; nor could he, like Grindal, find it probable that the truth, hidden from the world for fifteen centuries, had suddenly been revealed in the last few years to a group of important Englishmen. Elizabeth and Cecil had refused their co-operation in the Council of Trent.

England had been represented there, but by the dispossessed and fugitive Bishop Goldwell of St. Asaph. The continuity of English Catholicism survived, but in the secret, illegal congregations of the remote countryside and among the ever-growing colonies of refugees in Rome, the Netherlands, and the Channel ports. The official Anglican Church had cut itself off from the great surge of vitality that flowed from the Council; it was, by its own choice, insular and national. The question before Campion was, not whether the Church of England was heretical, but whether, in point of fact, heresy was a matter of great importance; whether in problems of such infinite magnitude human minds could ever hope for accuracy, whether all formulations were not, of necessity, so inadequate that their differences were of no significance. Tobie Matthew's way lay smooth before him; it was not on his responsibility that the changes had been made; perhaps they were regrettable, but, since that was the condition of the times, it was the duty of a loyal Englishman to throw in his lot with the Government and make the best of what was left. The new services were written in language which any man of culture might delight to enunciate; the points of variance, compared with the similarities, were not numerous. Campion loved his country and his countrymen; the way was easy for him to live among them in honour and authority; the ancient cathedrals were still standing, scarred and scoured perhaps, but fine prizes in the Government's gift—massive, visible tokens of unity with the past; titles of honour were still to be won which had been borne by the saints and scholars of antiquity. In a world where everything was, by its nature, a makeshift and poor reflection of reality, why throw up so much that was excellent, in straining for a remote and perhaps unattainable perfection?

It was an argument which might be—which was—acceptable to countless decent people, then and later, but there was that in Campion that made him more than a decent person; an embryo in the womb of his being, maturing in darkness, invisible, barely stirring; the love of holiness, the need for sacrifice. He could not accept.

Now, when Campion most required tranquillity in which to adjust his vision to the new light that was daily becoming clearer and more dazzling, events outside his control, both at Oxford and in the world at large, became increasingly obtrusive. Throughout the country discontent with Cecil's policy became consolidated. Under the Tudor system of government there was no place for a legitimate opposition; it was forced into conspiracy or rebellion. Leicester was deeply involved in intrigue with the Duke of Norfolk and the Conservative peers; this party, though led in part by Protestants and impelled primarily by feudal distaste for the Queen's low-born advisers, looked to the Catholics as their main source of support. At the same time the Government was drifting towards an antagonism to Spain which could only result in war. In the spring of '68 Mary Stuart took refuge and was imprisoned in England; in the winter the Queen confiscated a fleet of Spanish treasure ships which had put into harbour in Plymouth and Southampton, carrying half a million ducats to the Duke of Alva. England and Spain were confronted with precisely similar problems in Ireland and the Netherlands, and both had reason to fear the damage the other would do to them among their disaffected subjects. In the event of war abroad or rebellion at home, Cecil felt that the Catholics constituted a grave menace. They were proving more stubborn in their faith than had at first seemed likely. Books of controversy, printed by the English exiles abroad, were finding their way into the country in disturbing quantities; up till now the Catholics had spent little time in detailed argument; when in power, they had judged their opponents on the grounds of authority and obedience; now the old faith was being restated in new and persuasive terms, applicable to a generation who had grown up without the heritage of instinctive respect for tradition, terms of reason and research. It would have been easy to show lenience to a moribund superstition, the sentimental regrets of an old generation that was rapidly dying out; here was something unexpectedly vigorous and up to date, which must either suffer decisive and immediate defeat, or conquer. Accordingly, all over England the commissioners and magistrates were instructed to take a firmer line; at first no new legislation was used, but the law which before had been administered with some tact was everywhere more sternly enforced. More Catholics went into exile, among them Gregory Martin, Campion's closest friend for thirteen years, who had left Oxford to act as tutor in the Duke of Norfolk's family. The repression had begun which was to develop year by year from strictness to savagery, until, at the close of the century, it had become the bloodthirsty persecution in which Margaret Clitheroe was crushed to death between mill stones for the crime of harbouring a priest.

Campion, although a deacon and nominal member of

the Church of England, had made no secret of his spiritual wanderings; he had taken his doubts eagerly to anyone who he hoped might resolve them. He was not a reserved man; he loved argument; ideas, for him, demanded communication, and it was his particular genius to give them expression in lucid and memorable phrases. No one in Oxford can have been in any doubt of the way in which his mind was leading him.

But even had this not been his method; had he, instead, gone gravely about the duties of his office, lecturing, preaching, giving his advice at college meetings, and all the time waged a deep, interior argument, hearing anyone's views, never committing himself, until one day, his mind made up, he could startle his associates by a calm renunciation of all he had seemed to represent, he would have come under suspicion, now, when everyone watched his neighbour for signs of heterodoxy, by his familiarity with Richard Cheney of Gloucester.

It was in this bishop's library and at his table that half Campion's opinions were at this time formed. He was a virtuous, mild, learned, deeply embarrassed old gentleman of utterly different mind from his busy colleagues. He was the first high-churchman. His clergy regarded him as little better than a Papist, for he supported the Lutheran doctrine of consubstantiation, which affirmed the miraculous character of the Mass, and differed from Catholic teaching on points to which only metaphysicians could attend; he believed in the freedom of the will and the efficacy of good works, and was denounced for preaching 'very strange, perilous and corrupt doctrine, contrary to the Gospel'. He was excommunicated by his fellow-bishops. He employed against his opponents just those arguments from the Fathers and Councils which the Catholics could turn against him. Later from Douai, in 1572, Campion wrote to him one of his most eloquent letters, exposing the ignominy of his position.

> . . . You are sixty years old, more or less, of uncertain health, of weakened body, the hatred of heretics, the pity of Catholics, the talk of the people, the sorrow of your friends, the joke of your enemies. Against your conscience you falsely usurp the name of bishop, by your silence you advance a pestilential sect which you love not, stricken with anathema, cut off from the body into which alone the graces of Christ flow, you are deprived of the benefit of all prayers, sacrifices and sacraments. What do you think yourself to be? What do you expect? What is your life? Wherein lies your hope?

He urges him, with all the strength of his own new-found spiritual confidence, to make his surrender. But it needed more than a gentle heart and pious disposition to make a Catholic in that age; the old man stayed in his palace, increasingly lonely, maligned, distracted; deep in debt, sued by the Crown for 'tenths'; he died, as far as is known, undecided, and was buried without tomb or memorial in his own Cathedral; he was succeeded, first, by a dunce, next, by an absentee; the little work he had accomplished to preserve decency and toleration was quite undone, and thereafter there were few dioceses in England where the persecution was more ruthlessly pursued than in Gloucester.

Early in the gathering storm, pressure was brought upon Campion to declare himself. A part of his income was derived from an exhibition paid by the Grocers Company of the City of London. As rumours of his Popish sympathies began to spread, a demand was made by them that he should come to London and clear himself by preaching at St. Paul's Cross before Candlemas. At first Campion asked for a postponement, and the ordeal was put off until Michaelmas, when he would have had leisure to prepare his arguments. He was proctor at the time, an office which then involved heavy obligations in university and town. He resented this attempt of the city merchants to dictate to his conscience, and protested that declarations of the kind demanded were neither their business nor his; his duty lay at Oxford where he was a 'public person . . . charged with the education of divers worshipful men's children'. They suggested a less conspicuous place for his confession, the pulpit of St. Stephen's Church, Walbrook. He still refused and the Company accordingly deprived him of his exhibition.

There was no injustice in the sentence, nor did it involve any great hardship, for Campion was now in possession of a benefice given him by Cheney; he was fully alive to the ambiguity of his position, which was recognized as the first step towards taking Anglican Orders. It was daily becoming more difficult for him to remain in England. Gregory Martin was writing to him from Douai, urging him to leave, before he compromised himself further. On 1 August 1569, Campion's term of office as proctor came to an end. He punctually fulfilled his last duties, set things in order for his successor, and delivered the customary account of the year's work in his elegant, Ciceronian Latin. It was his last public act in the University.

He remained in residence at Oxford until the end of September 1570, and then he did not go at once to join Gregory Martin at Douai; he does not appear to have contemplated becoming a priest at all; he was not formally reconciled to the Church; by canon law he had put himself in a state of excommunication, and it is highly unlikely that, placed as he was, he could get into touch with anyone possessed of the necessary faculties to absolve him. He was, however, openly Catholic by conviction, and recognized as one by friends and opponents. It remained to be tried whether it was possible to readjust his life on this basis; whether there was any honourable life open to a Catholic layman. Only by slow stages was it revealed to Campion how complete was the sacrifice required of him. He had powerful friends and a brilliant reputation. Surely with these it must still be possible to make a career in the world, without doing violence to his religion? Surely it was not expected of him to give up *all*?

The present of a book turned his thoughts towards Ireland; it was from Richard Stanihurst, one of his most devoted pupils; the boy's own first composition, a commentary on Porphyry. Stanihurst's father was Recorder of Dublin and Speaker in the Irish House of Commons, a prominent man in the project, then on foot, to establish an Irish university. Here, it seemed, was an opportunity exactly suited to a man of Campion's attainments and antecedents. He was known to Sir Henry Sidney, the Lord Deputy. According to reports, the Reformation had, so far, made little stir in Dublin; laws of supremacy and uniformity had been enacted, but no great pains were taken to enforce them. Sidney was known to be tolerant, if not sympathetic, and, except for the Anglicized official class, everyone of importance still adhered to the old belief. Accordingly, with Leicester's approval, Campion repaired to Dublin, where he was warmly received by the Stanihursts. Sidney promised him protection from police interference. He was given lodgings in the Stanihursts' Dublin house. Besides Richard, there was a daughter who later married Ussher, a clerk of the Court of Chancery, and became mother of a future archbishop; and an elder brother, Walter, already married, but apparently living at home. The company they kept was drawn from the official Government class, partly civil servants sent out from England, partly the sons of Anglo-Irish families, most of whom had been educated across the Channel. They were on cordial terms with the neighbouring gentry, such as the Barnewells, and Richard later married one of the Barnewell daughters, thus allying himself to the Dunsanys and other prominent families of the Pale. Campion was accepted on terms of warm familiarity. At an early age his education had separated him from his own family; though he had two brothers of his own and a sister, they seem never to have played any part in his life; apparently he never had the inclination to marry; the schoolroom, the college dining-hall, the common room, the cloister, were his constant surroundings. He had seen something of the splendid, formidable life of the Court. With the Stanihursts, for the first and last time in his life, he tasted the happiness of a normal, cultured household. Here he shared the daily experiences of a busy and affectionate home circle; he enjoyed intelligent, topical conversation; there was a good library and a study set apart for him to work in, and, ahead, the promise of distinguished employment, when the projected university took form.

He settled in happily; he was at peace with his conscience, and, once more, on good terms with his surroundings. The ambition of serene scholarship and gentle, sympathetic society, so rudely disturbed at Oxford, seemed once more attainable; outside, beyond the mountains, among bog and rock, raged the tumultuous, tribal life of the Irish people, Geraldines, Butlers and McCarthys prosecuting their endemic feuds; here, apart from all that, apart from the rancorous jostling and the dark, high intrigues of the English Renaissance, lay the cosy, colonial world of the Pale; no hate, no bloodshed. . . .

He worked daily, coaching his old pupil, for his religion never overclouded his enthusiasm for learning and its rewards. 'Proceed with the same pains and toil,' he had written on receiving Richard Stanihurst's *Porphyry*, 'bury yourself in your books, complete your course . . . keep your mind on the stretch . . . strive for the prizes which you deserve. . . . Only persevere, do not degenerate from what you are, nor suffer the keen eye of your mind to grow dark and rusty.' With the project of the Irish university in his mind, he prepared a discourse *De Homine Academico,* an elaborate portrait of the ideal student. This paper has not survived in its original form, but we have an oration delivered shortly afterwards at Douai on the same subject, which was probably derived from it. Here he insists upon the virtues of piety, modesty, kindness, obedience, upon grace of deportment and civility of manners. The student's pronunciation must be specially cultivated, his mind 'subtle, hot and clear, his memory happy, his voice flexible, sweet and sonorous; his walk and all his motions lively, gentle-manly, and subdued'. His recreations are painting, playing the lute, singing at sight, writing music with facility and correctness. His first years at school are devoted to Latin, the rudiments of Greek, and the control of his own language, in which he must compose verses and epigrams. Later he must become a finished debater in philosophy, modelling himself upon Cicero; by his sixteenth year he must be able to write Greek iambics. He must master all histories, classical and modern, the ethics and politics of Aristotle and Plato, logic and natural science, so as to deserve the title of 'oracle of nature'. His habits of study must be regular and collected; he must not 'dull himself with unseasonable vigils' but allow seven hours' sleep at night and a proper attention to toilet and appearance. He must neither write licentious and amor-ous verses, nor fall into the puritanical extreme of eschewing the great literature of the past which occasionally bore this character. He must be a dialectician, an orator, an astron-omer, and in his last year of study a master of Hebrew. He must be respectful to his superiors, generous in judgement of his equals, courteous and helpful to the obscure. This catalogue no doubt defines the aim which Campion was setting himself and, to a great extent, realizing at this period.

Soon afterwards he began work on a history of Ireland. Recorder Stanihurst's library contained numerous uncol-lated scraps, journals, annals, books of correspondence; his conversation, too, was full of information of doubtful historical value. Campion knew no Gaelic; nor, probably, did anyone in his circle. His attitude towards the 'mere Irish' was derived from the people among whom he lived, who were confident of their own superiority and the beneficence of their rule; they spoke of the unadministered, alien territories almost exactly as their counter-types, the colonial officials of the nineteenth century, might speak of the bush lands of Africa; they retailed anecdotes of native savagery and superstition, and saw in English education the only cure for them; in Campion's own words, Ireland was 'much beholden to God for suffering them to be conquered, whereby many of their enormities were cured, and more might be, would themselves be pliable'.

The short history, begun at leisure but hastily scrambled together in the end, under pressing distractions, is remarkable as being Campion's only complete work which has survived in the English language. The rest of his published work was in Latin. The sermons, upon which his contemporary fame most depended, were never taken down, and we can only guess at their character from rare, fragmentary quotations. *The History of Ireland* is a superb piece of literature, comparable in vigour and rhythm to anything written in his day. With all its imperfections of structure and material, it is enough to show that, had Campion continued in the life he was then planning for himself, he would, almost certainly, have come down in history as one of the great masters of English prose. From the lovely cadence of the opening sentences, describing the physical character of the country which 'lieth aloof in the West Ocean, in proportion like an egg, blunt and plain at the sides, not reaching forth to sea in nooks and elbows of land as Britain doth', to the balanced, Ciceronian speeches at the end it is manifestly the work of a stylist for whom form and matter were never in conflict; there is no shadow of the effort and ostentation which clouds all but the brightest genius of the period.

Three extracts, chosen almost at random, must suffice to suggest the flavour of the work:

> The people are thus inclined: religious, frank, amorous, ireful, sufferable, of pains infinite, very glorious; many sorcerers, excellent horsemen, delighted with wars, great almsgivers, passing in hospitality. The lewder sort, both clerks and laymen, are sensual and loose to lechery above measure. The same, being virtuously bred up and reformed, are such mirrors of holiness and austerity, that other nations retain but a show or shadow of devotion in comparison of them.

> Clear men they are of skin and hue, but of themselves careless and bestial. Their women are well favoured, clear coloured, fair headed, big and large, suffered from their infancy to grow at will, nothing curious of their feature and proportion of body.

> 'Look, sir King; eye us well; it is not light prowess that has caused these valiant bodies to stoop. Scythians were we, and the Picts of Scythia—great substance of glory lodgeth in these two names.'

Campion's superiority to his contemporaries is well illustrated by comparing his work with another, anonymous, history written at about this time and collected later by Holinshed. They are both paraphrasing from the same chapter by Giraldus Cambrensis.

The one writes 'And here you may see the nature and disposition of this wicked, effrenated, barbarous and un-faithful nation who (as Cambrensis writeth of them) they are a wicked and perverse generation, constant always in that they are always inconstant, faithful in that they be un-faithful', and so on for the length of a column.

Campion renders it in two sentences: 'Covenant and indent with them never so warily, yet they have been found faith-less and perjured. Where they are joined in colour of surest amity, there they intend to kill.'

So easily, inevitably, through page after page of this little book, barely more than a pamphlet, the melodious phrases fall into place. What a translator for the Vulgate was lost in Campion!

The work was dedicated to Leicester—for Campion still looked to him as his patron—in an inscription of exquisite grace.

There is none that knoweth me familiarly, but he knoweth withal how many ways I have been beholden to your lordship. . . . How often at Oxford, how often at the Court, how at Rycote, how at Windsor, how by letters, how by reports, you have not ceased to further with advice, and to countenance with authority, the hope and expectation of me, a single student. Let every man esteem in your state and fortune the thing that best contenteth and serveth his imagination; but surely to a judgment settled and rectified, these outward felicities which the world gazeth on, are there and therefore to be deemed praisable when they lodge those inward qualities of the mind, which (saving for suspicion of flattery) I was about to say are planted in your breast. Thirteen years to have lived in the eye and special credit of a prince, yet never during all that space to have abused this ability to any man's harm; to be enriched with no man's overthrow, to be kindled neither with grudge nor emulation, to benefit an infinite resort of daily suitors . . . these are indeed the kernels for which the shell of your nobility seemeth fair and sightly. . . . This is the substance which maketh you worthy of the ornaments wherewith you are attired.

Admirable prose, redolent of the security and good humour in which it was written; tender, and big with promise for the future.

But this happy interlude proved brief and all the warm prospects illusory. A few subscriptions were raised for the new university; a site was suggested for it and a name— Plantolinum, in compliment of the Boleyn family; it was constantly discussed, but during the discussions it became clear that there were two parties in Dublin, on the one side Sidney, Stanihurst and Campion, on the other the Protestant clergy under the leadership of the Chancellor, Dr. Weston. The question was referred back to Cecil and nearly a generation elapsed before the scheme at last took form in the institution of Trinity College.

Anti-Catholic feeling, which at first had been scarcely

perceptible in Ireland, was brought into life by the events of the succeeding months.

In the winter of 1569 the rebellion of the Northern Earls had taken place in England; though feudal in essential character, it assumed a religious aspect when, as each place fell to the rebels, the Mass was restored there. Leicester had deserted the conspirators some time before; the Duke of Norfolk surrendered himself, and what had at one time threatened to be a widespread conservative reaction ended in a local adventure which never extended beyond a day's march of the traditional Percy and Neville territories; it was the last, forlorn protest of pre-Tudor chivalry. Mary Stuart was moved to the Midlands; the feudal levies melted away, and the Government forces settled themselves to a leisurely campaign of hanging in the affected areas. It had not caused serious alarm in Whitehall, but it had the effect of planting in the public mind the association of Catholicism with political treason which was to prove ineradicable for generations; the first sparks of that fierce and almost fatal conflagration which, stoked by Ridolfi and Guy Fawkes, was to smoulder on, through the Titus Oates conspiracy and the Gordon riots, almost until modern times.

In the spring of 1570 there occurred another event that completely recast the Catholic cause; Pope Pius V excommunicated the Queen. It is possible that one of his more worldly predecessors might have acted differently, or at another season, but it was the pride and slight embarrassment of the Church that, as has happened from time to time in her history, the See of Peter was at this moment occupied by a saint. Pius was a Dominican friar of austere observance and profound spiritual life; as the Duke of Alva complained, he seemed always to expect events in the world to take place without human agency. He chose a life of great loneliness; he lived in a little set of rooms removed from the great state apartments of the Vatican; he confided in no one and took counsel from very few; the Turks were threatening Christianity in the rear, her centre was torn by new heresies, his allies were compromising and intriguing, their purpose distracted by ambitions of empire and influence; in long vigils of silent, interior communion, Pius contemplated only the abiding, abstract principles that lay behind the phantasmagoric changes of human affairs. He prayed earnestly about the situation in England, and saw it with complete clarity; it was a question that admitted of no doubt whatever. Elizabeth was illegitimate by birth, she had violated her coronation oath, deposed her bishops, issued a heretical Prayer Book and forbidden her subjects the comfort of the sacraments. No honourable Catholic could be expected to obey her. The Emperor, the Duke of Alva, the King of Spain, were shocked at his decision. He consulted nobody; he acted without any regard to the events of the moment. He had heard of the rising of the Northern Earls and had been delighted with it; he did not know whether it had succeeded. Every government maintained its own secret lines of communication; his were far from efficient; it took three months or more for him to get a letter from England. He knew that there had been a rising, and that by now it was probably decided, one way or the other; rumours had, perhaps, reached Rome of its failure; he did not wait to hear them. The formalities were observed; in the first week of

Lent a Court of Inquiry heard the evidence of twelve trust-
worthy English witnesses; Elizabeth was charged and found
guilty on seventeen counts; on 12 February Pius pronounced
the sentence which on the 25th was embodied in the Bull
Regnans in Excelsis. Elizabeth was excommunicated and her
subjects released from the moral obligations of obedience to
her.

Three months later, on Corpus Christi Day, 25 May, a
manuscript copy of the document was nailed to the door of
the Bishop of London's palace, in St. Paul's Churchyard,
by Mr. John Felton, a Catholic gentleman of wealth and
good reputation. He was tortured and executed. On the
scaffold he made a present to the Queen of a great diamond
ring which he had been wearing at the time of his arrest,
with the assurance that he meant her no personal harm, but
believed her deposition to be for her own soul's good and
the country's. He was the first of the great company of
Englishmen who were to sacrifice their entire worldly prospects and their lives as the result of Pius V's proclamation.

His contemporaries and the vast majority of subsequent
historians regarded the Pope's action as ill-judged. It has
been represented as a gesture of medievalism, futile in an
age of new, vigorous nationalism, and its author as an in-
effectual and deluded champion, stumbling through the
mists, in the ill-fitting, antiquated armour of Gregory and
Innocent; a disastrous figure, provoking instead of a few
buffets for Sancho Panza the bloody ruin of English Catholicism. That is the verdict of sober criticism, both Catholic
and Protestant, and yet, as one studies that odd and compelling face which peers obliquely from Zucchero's portrait

at Stonyhurst, emaciated, with its lofty and narrow forehead, the great, beaked nose, the eyes prominent in their deep sockets, and, above all else, the serene and secret curve of the lips, a doubt rises, and a hope; had he, perhaps, in those withdrawn, exalted hours before his crucifix, learned something that was hidden from the statesmen of his time and the succeeding generations of historians; seen through and beyond the present and the immediate future; understood that there was to be no easy way of reconciliation, but that it was only through blood and hatred and derision that the faith was one day to return to England?

That year, at any rate, the Bull came most opportunely to Cecil. There was now the best possible evidence to confirm anti-Catholic feeling. He drew up the list of members for the new House of Commons and secured a body of uncompromising, Calvinistic opinion. Up till then Elizabeth had resisted his imposition of the Thirty-nine Articles; now she was forced to give way, and the Parliament won the first of their long series of Puritan victories over the monarchy. The measures against Catholics were tightened by another twist of the screw. Naturally enough, the importation of copies of the Bull was forbidden, but into the same Act a clause was introduced providing that 'if any person after the same 1st July should take upon him to absolve or reconcile any person . . . or if any shall willingly receive and take any such absolution or reconciliation' he incurred the penalties of high treason—execution and the confiscation of property. Gradually the discharge of the penal laws was put into new hands, and instead of the old-fashioned justices who usually knew and quite liked their Catholic neighbours and distrusted the innovations from Westminster, there rose to eminence a set of strict officials, party men put up by the Government with, at their back, a more odious rabble of spies and informers.

All this was reflected in Ireland, and, with Sidney about to retire, Campion's security became increasingly precarious. It was finally upset by the first brief incursion into serious history of the preposterous and richly comic figure of Mr. Thomas Stukeley. Even to the generation of Drake, Ridolfi and Hawkins he seemed a shady and irresponsible person, He was a middle-aged pirate of gentle West Country origin, who, in the spring of 1570, put into harbour at Vivero de Galicia in Spain and, calling himself a son of Henry VIII, offered to conquer Ireland for the Spanish throne. The King was but mildly interested in the suggestion; nevertheless, at request of an Englishwoman, sometime lady-in-waiting to Mary, the Duchess of Feria, with whom Stukeley had ingratiated himself, he consented to pay off the arrears of wages to Stukeley's crew, who had never expected to come to Spain, and were threatening mutiny. Stukeley hung about the Court and the Duchess's drawing-room all that year, but could persuade very few people to take him seriously; the ecclesiastics doubted the sincerity of his religious conversion, and refused to receive him into the Church; eventually Philip knighted him and sent him away, and for the time being he disappeared from diplomacy.

But the reports of his activity served Cecil, in the alarmed state of the country, as material for a scare of invasion in Ireland. The authorities in Dublin were instructed to arrest suspected Catholics, and at the beginning of March 1572 Campion, with his *History* still unfinished, became a fugitive. The Stanihursts took him out of town to the Barnewells at Turvey, a house naturally protected by water from surprise attack. There is no clear record of his movements in the next few months; he appears to have dodged back to Dublin in May, and from there to Drogheda; no doubt he lodged in the houses of various friends he had made, slipping away by night at news of the pursuivants' arrival, avoiding making any record that would be likely to incriminate his hosts. Finally, at the end of May, he embarked for England at the little port of Tredake, twenty miles from Dublin, disguised as a lackey and calling himself Mr. Patrick, in the service of Melchior Hussey, steward to Lord Kildare.

Before sailing, the ship was searched by police officers. Campion himself escaped detection, but they rifled his luggage and confiscated the manuscripts. Among them was the hastily completed *History*. There were other manuscript copies in existence, and eight years later, shortly before his removal from Prague, he was in correspondence to recover one of them; probably it arrived too late. He assumed that his own copy had been destroyed, but it lay about in various offices and passed from hand to hand until, some years after its author's death, it appeared, mutilated, in Volume II of Holinshed's *Chronicles*. As the ship gathered way and rolled through the stormy passage of the Irish Channel, Campion may well have seen in the loss of his book, with its elegant dedication to the Earl of Leicester, his final severance with the old life. Whatever achievement lay ahead of him was not to be the achievement at which he had once aimed; the glory, transcendent and undying, not what he had sought.

He spent a few weeks, unobtrusively, in England, and was in the crowd at Westminster Hall to witness the trial of Dr. Storey, a refugee whom Cecil had had kidnapped at Antwerp and brought home to suffer in old age under an insupportable charge of treason for the prominent part he had taken against the Protestants in Queen Mary's reign. The condemned man was executed on 1 June with peculiar ferocity; Cecil and the chief ministers stood close by while he was being disembowelled; the cries of agony made an agreeable theme for popular preachers such as Fulke, who quoted them as showing that their victim was 'manifestly void of patience, and no martyr, as the Papists did mightily boast of him'. But on that day Campion was in mid-Channel on his way to Douai. There was a check in his journey; his boat was stopped, and he was taken aboard the *Hare*, an English frigate, and so back to Dover, but the captain was more concerned to keep Campion's purse than get his prisoner to London, so they parted company at the coast. Campion travelled to some friends in Kent, raised some money, and eventually crossed to Calais without further interference.

PART II
THE PRIEST

THE PRIEST

The English College at Douai, to which Campion now went, had already, in the three years of its existence, become a rallying point for Catholic refugees of the most varying characters and antecedents. When the first emigration took place at Elizabeth's accession, the exiles had dispersed all over Europe, going wherever they saw the best chances of employment or support; but, from the first, the Spanish Netherlands had attracted the greatest number, both by reason of their accessibility from England and the connexions long established between the two countries by the wool trade. Several English scholars had been received at Belgian schools and cathedrals, and when Philip II carried out his father's project of founding a university at Douai, where his Flemish subjects might receive an education in their own tongue independent of French influence, an Englishman, Dr. Richard Smith of Merton, was made Chancellor, while later, another, Dr. Richard White, was made head of the law school established there by the Abbey of Marchiennes. Early in the history of the new university a house was formed for English students, where, in a very modest fashion, the great seminary had its origin.

The founder and first President was Dr.—later Cardinal —William Allen of Oriel, a gentleman of ancient Lancashire family, thirty-six years old at the date of the foundation,

1568, who had left Oxford at the first religious changes, become a priest in Louvain, and had already attracted notice as a controversialist in defence of the doctrines of purgatory and indulgences. The object of the College was primarily to supply priests for the Catholic population of England, for, since the bishops were all either in prison or under detention, it was impossible for them, except very rarely with the connivance of their gaolers, to ordain priests; the system of education imposed by the Government made it increasingly difficult to train candidates for orders in England; in a few years the Marian priests would begin to die out and, as Cecil foresaw, the old Church would quietly expire with them; that Catholicism did in fact survive—reduced, impoverished, frustrated for nearly three centuries in every attempt at participation in the public services; stultified, even, by its exclusion from the universities, the professions and social life; but still national; so that, at the turn of opinion in the nineteenth century, it could re-emerge, not as an alien fashion brought in from abroad, but as something historically and continuously English, seeking to recover only what had been taken from it by theft—is due, more than to any other one man, to William Allen.

His was a compelling and elaborate character. His prodigious power in human intercourse is clear from the uninterrupted success of the English College. He was dealing with men of every age and position; elderly ex-professors and heads of Houses; raw, embarrassingly enthusiastic converts; old-fashioned priests, schooled and ordained under the Marian régime, who came to him when they found their simple, rule-of-thumb dialectics insufficient to cope with their trained opponents; bitter fanatics whose fathers and brothers had died on the scaffold; later, when the seminary was recognized as a menace at Whitehall, spies, sent over by Walsingham to discover the secrets of the organization—all these it was Allen's task to sift out and control; to estimate their capabilities and vocations, to turn some to work writing tracts and translating, to keep some as lecturers and send some across the Channel to martyrdom. Besides them, there were at Douai an increasing number of Englishmen and women who regarded the College as their centre, and its President as their leader; some were passing through, others more or less permanently settled; great ladies like the widowed Countess of Northumberland; humble, homeless artisans—all looked to Allen for encouragement.

Throughout the whole period he was in constant anxiety about money and he was living among a foreign people. At Douai the exiles, at first popular enough, became, after a time, identified by the anti-Spanish faction with the viceregal Government; at Rheims, where he moved for a time, they were disliked as Englishmen. Only by unremitting caution could the students avoid becoming embroiled in the local disturbances. But never was the régime of the College interrupted; whatever doubts secretly harassed the President, however tumultuous the immediate circumstances, however desperate the future, everything went on as before, English and imperturbable.

Mass for the whole College was at five, all the priests celebrating daily; there was weekly confession and communion; twice a week they fasted, and even on ordinary days the fare was so meagre that two Belgians who had originally joined quickly removed elsewhere. The students were assumed to have some Latin before their arrival; they learned Greek and Hebrew; they took dictation from the Scriptures; during the course they went through the New Testament sixteen times. The teaching was counter-reformatory; in theology and exegesis they concentrated almost entirely upon controversial texts; in their spiritual exercises they were prepared for sacrifice; they were being trained not as scholars and gentlemen, but as missionaries and martyrs. Within a few years of its foundation the seminary was sending about twenty priests a year to England, of whom, before the end of Elizabeth's reign, 160 had died on the scaffold. To critics at the time this yearly dispatch to almost certain imprisonment or death, of relays of the finest youth of the Church, seemed a gruesome and intolerable waste. In 1584 the Jesuit General Aquaviva was to write that 'to send missionaries in order to give edification by their patience under torture might injure many Catholics and do no good to souls'. But Allen knew that the devotion of his seminarists, so gallantly squandered, sometimes, in a few weeks of ministry, was of more value than a lifetime of discreet industry. His was the humbler task of composing their epitaphs. One aim was paramount to him, whatever its cost; the Church of Augustine, Edward the Confessor, Thomas of Canterbury and Thomas More must go on.

But there was another side to Allen's activity; besides being a great university administrator, he was a man of affairs, the last of the English cardinal-politicians. There were unexplained absences, when, after a cautionary address, the President would leave his College for three months or so at

Rome; there was a voluminous correspondence, written in cipher, with the great men of the age, the Duke of Guise, the Cardinal of Como, Don John of Austria, with Philip himself; there were secret visitors, of whom the students knew nothing except the clatter of hooves and the appearance of strange liveries in the courtyard; there were Mr. Egremont Radcliffe and an anonymous poisoner who, at their several times, came to assassinate him; a sure sign, in that century, of political eminence.

From all these high affairs Allen's students were rigidly excluded. Political discussion was forbidden absolutely; Elizabeth's name was never mentioned in school or recreation, and in their lectures the Pope's deposing power might not be explained, even in hypothetical examples. As the door closed behind Sir Francis Englefield or the Papal nuncio, Allen would gather up the notes and cryptograms, the lists of disaffected noblemen, the tables tracing the descent of the Infanta Isabel-Clara from John of Gaunt, lock them away in his dispatch box and turn with equal mind to the kitchen accounts of the college refectory or to some particularly promising thesis which one of the tutors had left for his notice.

The end was single, but the means devious and distinct. In that regular and generous mind there was no confusion.

The College was still in its earliest phase at the time of Campion's arrival. It had not yet been granted the Papal subsidy which made possible the rapid expansion of the next few years. Seven priests and thirteen candidates for Orders, living sparsely and precariously, constituted the entire permanent community. Some were dependent on remittances sent out from England, others on grants from Philip and local patrons. There were other English students reading secular subjects at the university, who lived near the college and resorted to it for their religious and social needs. Visitors and refugees came and went. Probably the total number of English in Douai at this time varied between one hundred and one hundred and fifty.

For Campion exile from England meant reunion with many old friends. There was Gregory Martin, who had twice written him urgent invitations to accept the duty that was now thrust upon him, and Richard Bristow, of Exeter, who had appeared before Elizabeth in the same debate, and on the same side as Campion, during her memorable visit to the university. These two were to devote the rest of their lives to the College, leaving behind them the great Douai Bible, the most accurate English translation of the Scriptures that had then appeared. There were also Risdon, White, and Darell, all Oxford men, in whose sympathetic and appreciative company many of the asperities of exile disappeared.

For nearly two years Campion conformed to the congenial routine of the place. He read for his baccalaureate in Divinity, and at the same time acted as professor of rhetoric, delivering model orations on most of the important occasions of the year, and having as one of his pupils Cuthbert Mayne, who was to be the first martyr of the seminary priests. He received minor Orders, and, in the normal course, would have proceeded direct to the priesthood. Responsible work lay at hand for him at Douai, pamphleteering, lecturing, translating, the very tasks which he had sought in vain at Dublin, and from across the Channel the continuous, insistent summons to the highest destiny of all. The copy of the *Summa* which Campion was using at this time survives at Manresa College, Roehampton; it is annotated in his own hand and opposite an argument on baptism by blood occurs the single *mot prophète et radieux*, '*Martyrium*'. The persecution in England was still comparatively mild; the new Church attracted little enthusiasm, and the governing party proceeded with caution and reluctance; violent sentences were uncommon and, where they occurred, could more often be attributed to motives of personal greed than of religious intolerance. But none knew better than Dr. Allen the fate that lay ahead of his seminarists. So long as the Church seemed to be on her death-bed, Cecil was content to cut off the necessaries of her life and leave her to die in peace. Deprived of the sacraments, England would be lost to the Faith in a generation. But as soon as the young priests, now patiently conning their text books abroad, began to appear in their own country, to appeal to the old loyalties that lay deep in the heart of the people, to infuse their own zeal into the passive conservatism over which the innovators had won a victory too bloodless to be decisive, the character of the Government would change. Martyrdom was in the air of Douai. It was spoken of, and in secret prayed for, as the supreme privilege of which only divine grace could make them worthy.

But it was with just this question, of his own worthiness, that Campion now became preoccupied. There is no record of the date of his formal reconciliation with the Church, but it is reasonable to assume that it occurred immediately on his arrival from England. From then onwards he was admitted to the sacraments without which he had spent the past ten or twelve years of his life. From then onwards, for the first time in adult life, he found himself living in a completely Catholic community, and, perhaps for the first time, began to have some sense of the size and power of the world he had entered, of the distance and glory of the aim he had set himself. The faith of the people among whom he was now placed was no fad or sentiment to be wistfully disclosed over the wine at high table, no dry, logical necessity to be expounded in the schools; it was what gave them daily life, their entire love and hope, for which they had abandoned all smaller loyalties and affections; all that most men found desirable, home, possessions, good fame, increase, security in the world, children to keep fresh their memory after they were dead. Beside their devotion Campion saw a new significance in the evasions and compromises of his previous years. At Oxford and Dublin he had been, on the whole, very much more scrupulous of his honour than the majority; he had forsworn his convictions rarely and temperately; when most about him were wantonly throwing conscience to the winds and scrambling for the prizes, he had withdrawn decently from competition; but under the fiery wind of Douai these carefully guarded reserves of self-esteem dried up and crumbled away. The numerous small jealousies of university life, his zeal for reputation, his courtship of authority, the oaths he had taken of the Queen's ecclesiastical supremacy, the deference with which he had given assent to Cheney's view of conformity, his melodious eulogies of the Earl of Leicester, above all 'the mark of the beast', the ordination which he had accepted as an Anglican deacon, now appeared to him as a series of gross betrayals crying for expiation, fresh wounds in the hands and feet of Christ.

He had come to Douai as a distinguished immigrant. At the time of his departure Cecil remarked to Richard Stanihurst, 'It is a great pity to see so notable a man leave his country, for indeed he was one of the diamonds of England.' Allen received him as a sensational acquisition. He had left England, it may be supposed, in a mood of some pride and resentment; he was casting off the dust of ingratitude, taking his high talents where they would be better appreciated.

Now in this devout community, at the hushed moment of the Mass, he realized the need for other gifts than civility and scholarship; he saw himself as a new-born, formless soul that could come to maturity only by long and specially sheltered growth. There was now no question in his mind of finding scope for his abilities, but of preparing himself laboriously in self-knowledge and the love of God, to become capable of the lowest service. This could not be done at Douai among his old friends of the senior common-rooms, and, as his course of studies drew to their close, his mind turned more and more towards the selfless discipline and vigilance of the rule of St. Ignatius, to the complete surrender sought in the prayer *Suscipe, Domine, universam meam libertatem. Accipe memoriam, intellectum atque voluntatem omnem.* . . . Only thus, if ever at all, could he be worthy of the hangman and the butcher.

Accordingly, soon after he took his degree on 21 January 1573, he left for Rome with the intention, if God willed it, of entering the Society of Jesus. He travelled on foot, alone, as a poor pilgrim.

Allen did nothing to hinder him. A less spacious mind might have resented the decision. In its earliest years, with its prestige still uncertain, his College was losing its most notable convert; the community were bereft of a magnetic and inspiring companion; it was possible that Campion would be permanently lost to the English Mission, for there was no English Province in the Society and, although several English and Irishmen had joined the Society since its foundation, none had as yet been sent to work in their native countries. But to Dr. Allen the matter admitted of only one question: where would Campion best satisfy his particular spiritual needs? He knew that Douai had given him much, and that there was between them a bond of love and gratitude which separation could not weaken. His struggling mission was in need of everything, and he knew that Campion's prayers would be for them, whether he was dispatched to America or China, or confined for the rest of his days in the philosophy schools of Central Europe. Campion could help the English Mission best by realizing his own sanctity. The ways were involved and manifold, but the goal was one.

It was probably towards the end of February when Campion arrived in Rome. We do not know the exact date, nor have we much information about his life there until his departure at the end of June. We know that he visited Cardinal Gesualdi, was well received and offered preferment in the event of the Society deciding against his vocation. He had some conversation with the Cardinal on the subject of

the Bull *Regnans in Excelsis* which will be referred to later.
In his letters he mentions Father Ursnar and his old tutor,
John Bavand, as his chief benefactors at this time. It is recorded that he performed the customary devotions of the
pilgrimage with great zeal. He does not appear to have had
an audience at the Vatican.

Pius V had died early in the previous year, his last months
illuminated by the great victory of Catholic arms at the
battle of Lepanto. The danger which darkened the whole of
the period, that in its distracted state Europe might fall to
Islam, as North Africa and the Eastern Empire had fallen,
though still grave, was no longer desperate. Calvinism in
France and Lutheranism in Central Europe had reached their
widest expansion. The Tridentine reforms were becoming
effective in every branch of the Church's life. Pius's reign
ended, if not in triumph, in hope more substantial than had
been known for a generation. To the end he maintained his
energy and austerity. His last public appearance, a few days
before his death, was to make the arduous visit of the seven
churches; one of his last acts was to check this procession
in order to exchange a few words about their country with
some English pilgrims.

He was succeeded by Gregory XIII, a lawyer and efficient
man of affairs who had taken Orders late in life, after the
birth of an illegitimate son. He had then come into contact
with Borromeo and Philip Neri, and was profoundly in-
fluenced by the spiritual life which centred round them. He
took up the work of Pius, pursuing it with method and
discretion, reinforcing on all fronts the resistance to the
Turks and the Reformers. Under him the new Calendar was

introduced, which, denounced at first in all Protestant countries as an invention of anti-Christ, was gradually accepted in the subsequent two hundred years by each of them in turn. He was a friend of the Jesuits and remitted Pius's decree that they should sing the Office in choir, thus preserving for them one of the characters given by their founder, which particularly distinguished modern from medieval piety. In domestic government he encouraged a good standard of private morality by advancing men of orderly lives, but did not continue the more severe, puritanical measures of his predecessor under whom a wealthy layman had been publicly flogged for adultery and a drove of harlots turned loose on the campagna to be massacred by bandits. His chief minister was Galli, Cardinal of Como, who played a more important role in the foreign politics of the period than Pius allowed to any subordinate.

These two Popes, the saint and the administrator, may be taken to typify the change which had come over the Holy City, and was to determine her character through the succeeding centuries; the luxury and scepticism had gone, but with them something of the former chivalry and culture. The Popes were no longer patrons of art; their revenues were directed into strictly practical channels, to build missions and to subsidize theological colleges; their entourage ceased to be of courtiers and connoisseurs, but was composed, instead, of soft-footed, bureaucratic clergymen; no buffoon was kept in the Vatican after the Council of Trent to remind the Pontiff of his human follies; instead, at his elbow there was always a confessor.

At the time of Campion's visit to Rome the antiquities

were already out of favour. Both Paul and Pius had regarded pagan sculpture with detestation, and a large part of the Vatican collection had escaped destruction only by being bundled out of sight. The ruins, lately the resort of the dilettanti, which everywhere challenged the pilgrim's attention, were now valued by the moralist for their edifying witness to the mutability of human achievement. Archaeology found its place in the new order when, five years later, the first of the catacombs was excavated; here was something in the new fashion; all Rome crowded to the sunless galleries, promenading by candlelight between the interminable shelves of skeletons; scrawls were brought to light of first-rate controversial importance, affirming dogmas now in dispute, and were greeted with the enthusiasm which an earlier generation, secure in its orthodoxy, had squandered on the bronzes and marbles of ancient Greece.

A few years before, Campion might have found something to regret in the modern attitude, but now it commanded his whole sympathy. 'Make the most of Rome,' he wrote later to Gregory Martin. 'Do you see the dead corpse of that Imperial City? What can be glorious in life, if such wealth and beauty has come to nothing? But who has stood firm in these wretched changes—what survives? The relics of the Saints and the chair of the Fisherman.'

We do not know where he lodged; perhaps with Father Usnar. Writing, some years later, to John Bavand, he recalls the kindness he was offered and the spirit in which he received it. 'When I was in Rome did you not spend your entire self on me? On one from whom, to your knowledge, there could be no repayment; one just embarking from the world; in some sort, a dying man. It is a work of high compassion to bury the dead . . . you were munificent to me as I went to my rest in the sepulchre of religion.'

These words, heavy with the imagery of the Ignatian exercises, were written when he was a professed priest, but they may well represent the mood in which he accepted the weeks of delay. In his mind he eagerly anticipated the noviciate; it was no reluctance on his part which held him in Rome, but the circumstance that the third General of the Jesuits, Francis Borgia, had recently died and that the congregation was assembled to elect his successor.

The Society had now been in existence nearly thirty-three years, and in that time had drawn to itself men from every degree of life—Faber the shepherd, Borgia the Duke of Gandia, Polanco the Jew. The first three Generals had been Spanish, but the membership included nearly every nationality; there had been several Englishmen, Br. Lambert, a lay brother in the time of Ignatius Loyola, Fr. Darbyshire, Fr. Good, Fr. Heywood, all three Oxford men with whom Campion probably had some acquaintance, Fr. Rastall, a great nephew of Sir Thomas More, and others. The Society knew no bounds to its work but those of the human race; its missionaries penetrated to India, China, Japan, Abyssinia and the New World; in the lecture halls of the ancient universities, in obscure provincial day schools, guarding the consciences of great ladies at Court and of dying seamen on the bullet-swept decks at Lepanto, among galley-slaves and lepers. in council with Cardinals and men of affairs, wherever there were souls to be saved, these men of single purpose were making a way.

In government the Society was, and is, a highly central-
ized autocracy under a General, elected for life; by the con-
stitutions he is chosen not for any pre-eminent intellectual
attainments or influence, but for 'the habit of union with
God' and experience in the Society's affairs. An Admonitor
is appointed with him to be always at hand supervising and,
when necessary, correcting his private conduct. He is resident in Rome, and direct to him come reports of the
Society's work from all parts of the world; from him issue
appointments and orders. The congregation which elects
him consists of the Provincial of every Province accompanied by two priests chosen by their fellows.

As has been stated above, the congregation, thus composed, was assembled in Rome by the beginning of the year
1573, and after it had elected a Fleming, Mercurianus, as
General, on 23 April it proceeded among other business to
review the candidates for entry and apportion them to their
respective Provinces. No difficulty was made about Campion's reception—indeed his biographers claim that there
was some competition for him—and it was eventually decided that he should join the Austrian Province under Fr.
Magius. He was offered the series of questions addressed to
every postulant:

> Are you willing to renounce the world, all possessions
> and all hope of temporal goods? Are you ready if neces-
> sary to beg your bread from door to door for the love
> of Jesus Christ? Are you ready to reside in any country
> and to embrace any employment where your superior
> may think you to be most useful to the glory of God

and the good of souls? Are you willing to obey in all things in which there is evidently no sin, the superiors who hold towards you the place of God? Do you feel resolved generally to renounce without reserve all those things which men in general love and embrace, and will you attempt and desire with all your strength what our Lord Jesus Christ loved and embraced? Do you consent to put on the livery of humiliation worn by Him, to suffer as He did and for love of Him, contempt, calumnies and insults?

He assented and was received as a novice.

In the middle of June the congregation dispersed, and Campion, in company with certain Spanish and German Fathers, travelled with his Provincial to Vienna, where they arrived in August. The noviciate was stationed at Prague, where, accordingly, Campion was now sent in company with Father James Avellanedo, the newly chosen confessor to the Empress. After two months there he was moved to Brunn in Moravia with five other novices, where he remained until September 1574, when he was again removed to Prague, which was to be his home for the succeeding six years.

It was no part of the Jesuit system to station its forces in remote or congenial country. Other religious Orders, training their members for other ends, have built their houses in the desert, on cliffs and desolate promontories above the sea, or high in secluded valleys where crest upon crest of tranquil upland stretch uninterrupted to the horizon and dispose the mind to peace. The Jesuits' work lay in the crowded cities, wherever the conflict was hottest and the issue least sure, and it was for these very reasons that Prague and Brunn were chosen for the Austrian noviciate.

Until the Hussite disorders at the beginning of the preceding century, Prague had been the centre of Middle Europe for scholarship and culture. Inspired by Wycliffe, John Huss taught that 'Universities, studies, degrees, colleges and professorships are pagan vanities, and of no more use to the Church than the devil', and during his brief period of eminence he was able to reduce the ancient university to ruin. Like the culture which it fostered, the university was international. Appealing to the particularist sentiment, in which the reformers of the next century were to find their chief support, Huss succeeded in driving out the foreign students who formed the strength and life of the place. To the number of several thousand they left the country and founded the University of Leipsic, while Huss was left rector over a few hundred Bohemians. This easy success tempted him to greater energy in the denunciations of Catholic teaching and organization, which he had already begun from the pulpit of the Bethlehem Church. His counsels made for disorder rather than revolution, for, unlike Calvin and Luther, he suggested nothing to replace the system which he was attacking, and his conformity with some points of Catholic doctrine was as capricious as his dissent from others. But his supporters, by the prerogatives which he himself affirmed, were at liberty to select and amplify whatever they found personally sympathetic in his teaching. His execution at Constance inflamed the anti-clerical and anti-royal sentiment of the Bohemian nobility who were soon at war with their king and with one another. Hostilities, lasting fifteen years, impoverished the country and resulted in a decisive defeat to the extremists and a treaty generally acceptable to the more moderate reformers. The monarchy, however, was fatally weakened, became elective, and finally, in 1526, passed into the hands of Charles V, who absorbed it into the Empire. Fifty years of comparative peace followed, but the university never recovered its dignity.

Lutheran teaching achieved an immediate popularity, and at the time of the Jesuits' arrival there the country was predominantly, if apathetically, Protestant. They came, at the Emperor's invitation, to take up the Church's battle on a losing front.

From the time of Ignatius until the present day the Jesuit's training has retained its essential structure. The postulant is assumed to have attained a respectable standard of education before admission. For the two years of his noviciate his studies cease, and he devotes himself entirely to a routine designed to develop the character in holiness and obedience, after which he takes his first vows and resumes his studies for the priesthood. Campion, with his ample attainments in philosophy, rhetoric and divinity, was able to complete the course in five years, and said his first Mass on 8 September 1578.

His exterior life during these five years is easily told. The routine was hard, but without the extreme physical austerities of some other systems. The first month of the noviciate, following the precept from which there has been no deviation, was spent in absolute solitude; here, disturbed by no human intercourse except that of his director, he followed the *Spiritual Exercises,* in meditation and scrupulous examination of conscience, and erased all previous experience in a detailed confession of his whole life. He then resumed the companionship of the other novices and shared with them the manual labour of the household, of which he has left an enthusiastic description in a letter written from Prague after he had become a professed priest.

> How could I help taking fire at the remembrance of that house [Brunn] where there were so many burning souls—fiery of mind, fiery of body, fiery of word with the flame which God came upon earth to send, that it should burn there always? O dear walls, that once enclosed me in your company! Pleasant recreation-room, where we talked so holily! Glorious kitchen, where the best of friends—John and Charles, the two Stephens, Sallitzi, Finnit and George, Tobias and Gaspar—fight for the pots in holy humility and charity unfeigned! How often do I picture it; one returning with his load from the farm; another from market; one sweating, sturdy and merry, under a sack of refuse, another toiling along on some other errand! Believe me, my dearest brethren, your dust and brooms, chaff and loads are beheld with joy by the angels. . . . Would that I had never known any father but the fathers of the Society; no brothers but yourselves and my other brothers; no business but that of obedience; no knowledge but Christ crucified.

At Brunn their work brought the novices into frequent contact with the Moravians round them, who, like the

Bohemians, were for the most part disaffected in religion. It was hoped that the enthusiasm of the Jesuits in their midst might prove infectious, and the young novices, following the classic 'Experiments', were sent out to converse with them, begging from door to door, labouring in the hospitals and sick rooms, and tramping among the outlying villages to teach the catechism to children. This work, whose importance the Bishop of Olmütz particularly urged, brought back some converts, but not in any remarkable number, and it soon became clear to the Provincial that his end would best be served by opening in that part of the Empire one of the schools which were already becoming famous throughout Europe. He chose Prague for its seat; accordingly, in September 1574, Campion was recalled there, and became Professor of Rhetoric, the first of a series of important posts which he held at the new school.

From now, until his summons to Rome in 1580, Campion's activities were entirely educational. The Jesuits may fairly be said to have created a new system in teaching; their schools were the best equipped and the best staffed; their text books were the most modern and their curriculum the widest, but, more than anything else, it was their classroom method that won them the supremacy which they enjoyed throughout Europe from this period until the eve of the French Revolution, so that even at times of the sharpest religious difference Protestant parents could be found sending their sons to them. Their own acute training gave them particular insight into the habits of the mind, and to them may be credited the discovery and application of the principle, now universally accepted, that a pupil will be able to retain more in his memory when he has acquired it in a mood of curiosity and imagination. However admirable the higher achievements of medieval scholarship, its primary and secondary education had been pedestrian; a matter of teaching by rote an unvaried syllabus of rules and citations, and of enforcing defective attention with the rod; the facts and principles of knowledge were treated as the stones, laboriously laid, of a work whose nature would appear only towards the end of the building. The Jesuits sought to present everything as having an immediate significance and intrinsic interest; they fostered competition and argument with the result that the driest grammatical questions became the subjects of hot debate. Wherever they went they encouraged oratory and acting; they paid particular attention to style of language and dexterity of wit, but chose the material of their exercises so that, in the course of them, knowledge was acquired almost without effort.

During his six years at Prague, Campion worked tirelessly in the community and in the school. He was Professor of Rhetoric and later Professor of Philosophy, Praefectus Morum, Praefectus Cubiculi, Director of the Sodality of the Immaculate Conception, and Latin preacher; he gave frequent displays of oratory and wrote and produced plays, some of great length, for all important occasions. When he became a priest, he was in great demand in the town as preacher and confessor, and still found time for visiting the prisons and hospitals. It became the fashion to employ him for important funeral orations. In 1577 a tragedy of his, on the subject of Saul, was produced with great splendour at the expense of the municipality before Elizabeth, the widow of

Charles IX of France; it played for six hours, and was repeated next day at the request of the Emperor.

During this time he received the news of six of his Oxford friends entering the Society, but the only Englishman with whom he appears to have had any contact (besides Father Ware, who was at the college with him), is Philip Sidney, who arrived in 1576 as English Ambassador to congratulate the Emperor Rudolph on his accession. It was natural that he should call upon Campion, who had been an associate of his father's in Dublin, and as a fellow-Englishman living near the centre of local affairs would be able to supply him with much information of the kind which Walsingham required, but he was embarrassed to do so openly for fear of the spies who had already made mischief for him at the time of his visit to Venice. They did meet, however, more than once, and enjoyed long and serious discussions. Campion was left with the conviction, whether as a result of Sidney's impressionable nature or merely of his engaging manners, that his visitor was at heart a Catholic and solicited John Bavand to pray for 'the poor, wavering soul' of the magnificent young Englishman.

He kept up a correspondence, of which part has survived, with and about his old friends and pupils. The references to English affairs are rare. No doubt his unhappy country was frequently in his prayers, but, as far as his own life lay, the severance seemed complete; the probability was that he would remain at Prague until his death, following the same routine year after year, extending himself to the utmost in the work that lay immediately at hand. During his last months at Prague he was engaged in procuring a copy of his *History of Ireland,* with the intention of revising it and preparing it for publication.

These were the externals of his Jesuit vocation; of the other, interior life, the penances and rapt meditation, the prayer and communion, the inner struggles and victories, we know nothing except as their results appear in his life. To the superficial observer there might seem to be little change. He was leading the old life which he knew and loved, living in a celibate community, maturing and polishing his scholarship, instructing, expounding, disputing as he had done before, more tenderly, perhaps, and more thoroughly, without trace of vanity and emulation, but to all appearances much the same man as he had been at Oxford and Dublin. The precise discipline of the Ignatian *Exercises* had served only to confirm him in the habit of life he had originally chosen.

Then comes the interruption, for the origin of which it will be necessary to notice some recent events in Rome, and Campion suddenly emerges as a hero.

It was an age replete with examples of astounding physical courage. Judged by the exploits of the great adventurers of his time, the sea-dogs and explorers, Campion's brief achievement may appear modest enough; but these were tough men, ruthlessly hardened by upbringing, gross in their recreations. Campion stands out from even his most gallant and chivalrous contemporaries, from Philip Sidney and Don John of Austria, not as they stand above Hawkins and Stukeley by finer human temper, but by the supernatural grace that was in him. That the gentle scholar, trained all his life for the pulpit and the lecture room, was

able at the word of command to step straight into a world
of violence, and acquit himself nobly; that the man, capable
of the strenuous heroism of that last year and a half, was
able, without any complaint, to pursue the sombre routine
of the pedagogue and contemplate without impatience a
lifetime so employed—there lies the mystery which sets
Campion's triumph apart from the ordinary achievements
of human strength; a mystery whose solution lies in the
busy, uneventful years at Brunn and Prague, in the profound
and accurate piety of the Jesuit rule.

The letter which first informed Campion that he was
going to England came from Dr. Allen, and in order to
understand the circumstances of the mission it is necessary
to review some of the events which had occurred in the lives
of the English immigrants at Douai and Rome since his
departure. Cardinal Allen's college had increased greatly in
size and importance, and was now in receipt of a large
Papal subsidy which enabled it to support an average
membership of rather more than a hundred. Thirty or forty
priests were ordained yearly, more than half of whom
managed to cross the Channel into England, from where
they sent reports of the great enthusiasm with which they
were received by people of all classes, the hunger for the
sacraments which still survived, and the eagerness with
which they were sought by penitents desiring reconciliation. As a result of their labours, more Englishmen every
year were coming abroad with the intention of becoming
priests. It was to deal with some of this immigration that
Pope Gregory decided to found an English seminary in

Rome. There already existed a pious foundation of the Middle Ages, the Hospice in the Via di Monserrato, which housed numerous English exiles; it was now proposed to amplify this and create a regular seminary on the lines of Douai. The matter was put in the hands of Dr. Owen Lewis, sometime Fellow of New College, later a colleague of Allen's at Douai, Canon of Cambrai, a distinguished jurist, who was in Rome at the time on legal business for his Chapter. Despite his education at Winchester and Oxford and his long sojourn abroad, Dr. Lewis still retained a predominant devotion to his native Wales, and a wistful, Celtic strain in his character, which made him uneasy among the rigid Tridentine clergy who surrounded him. At his and Bishop Goldwell's suggestion a fellow-Welshman, Dr. Morys Clynog, was appointed Rector, a kindly, chatty, homesick, old man, whose emotional patriotism was not balanced, as in Dr. Lewis, by very weighty scholarship. Up to this time he had been in charge of the old-fashioned English Hospice where neither his discretion nor business ability had been very severely taxed. He had a deep affection and loyalty to men of his own blood, and it was his great joy to welcome them to the College; by 1579 he was able to number seven Welshmen among his students, with most of whom, in his Celtic enthusiasm for genealogy, he was able to claim personal kinship. For the thirty-three Englishmen who composed the remainder of the community he could feel only the most tepid sympathy.

The greater part of these had been sent to him from Douai, for during the years 1576-9 the position of the English students in the Netherlands had become insecure.

The Spanish Government was faced with a situation very similar to that which confronted Elizabeth in Ireland, and her advisers, despite her own expressed reluctance, had been quick to provide the Prince of Orange with help of the kind which later Philip was to give to the Earl of Desmond. The Calvinists in Douai were a small minority, but the richly deserved unpopularity of the Spanish garrisons aided their cause. The English students, being under direct Papal and royal patronage, and being moreover physically defenceless, found themselves an easy target for popular insult. The streets of the town became dangerous to them. It soon became clear that they would have to find a temporary home elsewhere. Cardinal Allen, accordingly, took as many of them as was possible into French territory at Rheims and sent the remainder to Rome.

These young martyrs in training were of different mettle from the ordinary, docile seminarists of the Roman colleges, and the unremitting tact by which Dr. Allen managed to keep them all harmoniously at work was attested by their behaviour as soon as they were removed from his control.

At the end of October 1578 two Italian Jesuits—Fathers Navarola and Capecius—were added to the staff of the Roman college; the English students could not fail to contrast their up-to-date efficiency with the slipshod, ramshackle mentality of their Rector, nor could the Fathers fail to prefer their keen-witted, generous English pupils to the moody Celts, but there is no reason to believe that they had any share in encouraging the disorders. The endemic antagonism of Welsh and English which, as the malcontents naïvely remarked in a petition to the Holy Father, dated from the days of King Arthur, was inflamed by the shameless advantage which the Rector gave to his countrymen in anything that lay in his power: better food, better rooms, better clothes. The English were soon in open rebellion; the ringleaders marched to the Pope, and were refused admission; they went to the Cardinal of Como, who referred them to Cardinal Morone; Cardinal Morone told them to go back to their books. Accordingly, after a scene in the dining-hall, which came near to bloodshed, the whole body of them, at the beginning of Lent 1579, marched out, with the intention of making their way back to Dr. Allen at Rheims. The Jesuits openly sympathized with them, and began raising a collection to provide for their journey. At this juncture the Pope intervened and promised a change of management. They asked first for Dr. Morton or Dr. Bavand as Rector, but were refused; they then suggested the Jesuits, and this was allowed them; for nearly two hundred years the college remained under the control of the Society; an Italian, Father Agazzari, was the first Rector.

Allen was invited to Rome to help in the settlement. The disturbance had caused great anxiety to him and to Dr. Lewis, though it is typical of this godly man that he had made no reproach to the students for their ingratitude to himself, who had been the chief benefactor of the College, but was distressed only at the scandal that might be caused and the danger to the students if they undertook the journey to Rheims without proper precautions. Dr. Allen was on the whole in favour of entrusting the College to the Jesuits, but in the three months of his journey south, the temper of the students was again excited against their authorities.

This time the complaint was more sober: that the Fathers, by their superiority to their predecessors, were gaining too great an influence over the more zealous students and would end by turning them into Jesuits instead of into English priests. Allen had already seen several of his most promising students, Campion among them, drawn into the Society away from direct participation in the English mission. In each case he had submitted, thinking it was for the individual's highest good, but it was another matter to expose an entire seminary college to this influence. If there was to be extensive recruiting for the Society among his students, it was fair that they should take their part in the work in England. In a series of long discussions with the General and the superiors of the Society, Allen pleaded his case and secured their agreement. In future English Jesuits should co-operate with Allen's priests, and arrangements were made for the immediate disposal of two Fathers for the next mission. On 5 December he wrote with great joy to inform Campion that he was one of those who had been chosen to go:

> Our harvest is already great in England: ordinary labourers are not enough; more practised men are wanted, but chiefly you and others of your Order. The General has yielded to all our prayers; the Pope, the true father of our country, has consented; and God, in whose hands are the issues, has at last granted that our own Campion, with his extraordinary gifts of wisdom and grace, should be restored to us.

It was not until March that the Austrian Provincial would allow his departure. In the time of waiting Campion continued without interruption in the normal order of the school, but there was the aura about him of one devoted to another destiny. A Silesian Father, James Gall, an ecstatic, came to the door of Campion's cell, on the eve of his departure, and inscribed above it *P. Edmundus Campianus Martyr*. Some days before another Father had painted the emblem of martyrdom, a garland of roses and lilies, on the wall at the head of Campion's bed.

Campion left Prague on 25 March, and travelling sometimes on foot, sometimes on horse, sometimes by coach, as the chances of the journey allowed, arrived in Rome on Easter Saturday, 9 April 1580. He remained there until 18 April. During this time he made or renewed the acquaintance of his companions on the mission. Of these by far the most important both in Campion's life and the future history of his generation was the fellow-Jesuit, Robert Persons. They had met before at Oxford, and had lately exchanged letters. At their first encounter Campion had been proctor and Persons, as an undergraduate, six years his junior, had been required by the university rules to take the Oath of Allegiance and Supremacy before him. He was known to have Catholic sympathies, and Campion had been ready to excuse him, but other authorities intervened and Persons took the oath, which he was to repeat later on becoming Fellow of Balliol. He was now, at Campion's earnest request, appointed his superior during their mission.

The materials for writing a life of Persons are not yet accessible, and until that day is thought to have arrived he must remain a shadowy and enigmatic figure. The little that is known of him is mostly derived from the utterances of his enemies. He was humbly born at Nether Stowey in Somerset. He was educated by the help of the parish priest, first at Taunton and later at St. Mary's Hall, Oxford, where he showed acute intelligence, if not scholarship, and inspired very strong feelings in all he met, either of affection or dislike. In 1574 he was obliged to resign his Fellowship in circumstances of which religion had no share. He had apparently succeeded in antagonizing the other dons by his popularity as a tutor and the licence he allowed himself in ridiculing them, but there is no reason to suppose that the charges which brought about his dismissal, of misappropriating college funds, were ever proved. He went to Padua to study medicine, but on the way stopped at Louvain, where he encountered Father William Good, under whose direction he seems to have experienced a profound and permanent conversion. He left Padua for Rome, entered the Jesuit noviciate on 24 July 1575, and was ordained priest there three years later. He became Penitentiary at the Vatican, where he rapidly attracted the notice of his superiors, and was employed for a short time at the English College in the transition period between Clynog's administration and the assumption of management by the Society. After Campion's death he never returned to England, but busied himself in ecclesiastical and secular politics, in which his projects were seldom wholly successful. Legends inevitably accumulated about him, magnified by the extreme expressions of his friends and enemies; and in the vague and slightly sinister form in which he has descended to posterity he forms the prototype, rarely repeated, of the 'subtle Jesuit' of popular superstition.

It seems certain that in later life he interpreted very loosely the strict Jesuit rule against interference in politics; he seems, too, to have worked under the conviction that all affairs, civil and ecclesiastical, could be more efficiently and conveniently managed by the Fathers of the Society. As a politician he proved wrong, but often, apparently, through ill-luck rather than bad judgement, as when the Raid of Ruthven upset his plans in Scotland; as an ecclesiastic he ended by antagonizing a great body of the more responsible clergy. But in all these matters the details, and perhaps the true facts, are hidden from us. We do know, however, that he completely captivated a man as astute in his human judgements as Dr. Allen; that he founded the school for English boys at St. Omer, which preserved Catholic education for three centuries of Englishmen and is the direct ancestor of Stonyhurst College, and that he composed the *Spiritual Directory*, which has proved a text book of sturdy piety to thousands of Catholics up to the present day.

In the few days of preparation and leave-taking which succeeded Campion's arrival in Rome, the purpose on which they were being sent was fully and precisely explained to the two missionaries. A large part of their instruction was concerned solely with their vocation as members of the Society, for it had been the chief anxiety of the General, which had for so long made him hesitate in his decision to send men to England, how it would be possible to lead the life of a Jesuit in the peculiar conditions that prevailed there. They would be obliged to abandon their habits and travel in disguise, living among laymen under assumed names and false professions of their business; they would be alone for long periods of time, entirely deprived of the corporate strength which was the chief advantage of membership of an organized Society; they would be without supervision and direction in a country where the ecclesiastical government had fallen into chaos and the only surviving bishop lived in imprisonment; they would be hindered, if not absolutely prevented, from making the periodic retreats in which they recuperated their spiritual powers. But the General had decided to commit them to these dangers, and accordingly he drew up a special code of rules for their work.

The objects of the mission were clearly defined and limited. It was for 'the preservation and augmentation of the faith of the Catholics in England'. So far from active proselytizing among heretics, the missionaries were charged not only to avoid disputes with them, but to shun their company. They might treat with Catholics who had lapsed through compulsion or ignorance, but this work was subordinate to their primary duty of ministering to those who remained constant. They were forbidden, absolutely, to involve themselves in questions of state or to send back political reports. They must permit no conversation against the Queen in their presence, except perhaps in the company of those whom they held to be exceptionally faithful, and who had been tried a long time; and even then not without serious cause. At this point a definition was required by the Fathers of the precise position of Catholics towards Queen Elizabeth. As early as 1573, during his first visit to Rome, Campion had had some conversation with Cardinal Gesualdi and had represented to him the difficulty in which loyal Englishmen had been placed by the Bull of Deposition.

After Pius's death an inquiry had been sent to Rome to discover whether the Bull was still in force, and had elicited
the following replies: that it had been issued in the hope of
the kingdom being immediately restored to Catholicism,
and in view of that occasion, and that as long as the Queen
remained *de facto* ruler, it was lawful for Catholics to obey
her in civil matters and co-operate in all just things; that she
might honourably be addressed with her titles as Queen;
that it was unlawful for any private person, not wearing
uniform and authorized to do so as an act of war, to slay
any tyrant whomsoever, unless the tyrant, for example, had
invaded his country in arms; that in the event of anyone
being authorized to put the Bull into execution, it would
not be lawful to Catholics to oppose him. These judgements
were now confirmed and epitomized in the statement 'that
the Bull should always bind the Queen and the heretics; on
the other hand that it should in no way bind the Catholics,
as things then stood, but only in the future when the public
execution of the Bull could be made'.

It was possible to deduce from this decision that the
Catholics were a body of potential rebels, who only waited
for foreign invasion to declare themselves. This was the
sense in which Cecil read it, for he was reluctant to admit the
possibility of anyone being both a patriotic Englishman and
an opponent of his régime. The Catholics, however, concerned very little with matters of high politics and very
much with their ordinary day-to-day relations with their
neighbours, accepted it eagerly, as permission to deny the
royal authority only in so far as it forbade them the practice
of their religion, and in all other matters to arrange their

lives in harmony with their fellow-countrymen. It was in this sense only that the question interested Persons and Campion. It was the very antithesis of their mission to instruct Catholics in their duty in the hypothetical event of King Philip suddenly appearing among them at the head of a victorious army; they came to treat with distressed consciences, and Gregory's pronouncement enabled them to reassure scrupulous penitents who feared that by performing the normal duties of citizenship they had incurred the penalities of excommunication.

A lay brother of the Society, Ralph Emerson, was appointed to accompany the two Fathers. With him, the party leaving for England now numbered fourteen, and represented all ranks of the Church; there was the aged Bishop Goldwell of St. Asaph, who with Dr. Morton, the Penitentiary of St. Peter's, travelled ahead by horseback; there were two laymen, one of them John Pascal, a young gallant who had lately been hanging about the Vatican and making himself noticeable by his debonair manner; four elderly Marian priests from the English Hospice, one of them the old Prior of Manchester; and three young priests from the college; so that the expedition began to assume the air of a crusade. Before leaving they were received in audience by the Pope, and given special faculties for their work; they also visited Philip Neri and received his blessing. When the actual day for their departure came, they were attended by Sir Richard Shelley, the Prior of Malta, and almost the whole of the English colony of Rome, as well as a large number of Italian sympathizers, as far as the Ponte Molle, where solemn and affectionate leave was taken. These circumstances, far from unobtrusive, were duly notified to Walsingham by his agents, and the English Government was well aware what was on hand before the missionaries had reached the Channel ports.

The first ten days of the journey were accomplished in heavy rain and over roads which were barely passable. The way led through Viterbo, Siena, Florence, Bologna, Modena, Parma, Piacenza and Milan. At Siena and Florence they were able to obtain lodging at Jesuit colleges; at Bologna, where they were delayed some days by an accident to Persons, they were entertained by Cardinal Paleotto, the Archbishop; after dinner Campion was called upon to preach, which he did in his old academic manner, beginning with a quotation from Pythagoras, and comparing the ardours and consolations of the Christian life with those of the pagan.

At Milan they spent eight days in the palace of Cardinal Borromeo, where a daily discourse was required of Campion. That huge and princely establishment was well accustomed to visitors of every degree; it numbered over a hundred members of the regular household; there were Chamberlains, Almoners, Stewards, Monitors, Oblates, Discreets of the Confraternity, Prefects of the Guest Chambers, all maintained and graded in hierarchic order under the Praepositus, the Vicar and the Auditor-General. Three hundred guests a month, on an average, passed through these hospitable courts; there all the ways and passages of the vast, ecclesiastical labyrinth seemed to intersect, and in the centre of it all, living in ascetic simplicity among the lavish retinue, eating his thin soup, sleeping on his folding

bedstead, wearing his patched hair shirt, moving with halting gait, chilly even in the height of summer, speaking in a
voice so subdued that it was barely audible, grave and recol-
lected as a nun, was the dominating figure of the great
Cardinal. The pilgrims were received, entertained, blessed
and sent on their way, and the immense household went
about its duties; in its splendour and order and sanctity, a
microcosm of the Eternal Church.

From Milan the party passed through Turin, crossed the
Alps by the Mont Cenis hospice, and descended into Savoy,
where they met the vanguard of a great rabble of Spanish
troops, returning from Flanders. They pressed on as far as
Aiguebelle, where it became clear that they would have to
change their course, for not only was there a continuous
stream of soldiers blocking the roads and commandeering
provisions, but, they learned, the country round Lyons was
in a state of anarchy as a result of the Huguenot rebellion.
Accordingly they struck east of their original route, along
the road through Geneva. As they approached the home of
Calvinism, they put out of sight all evidence of their profession and disguised themselves, Campion with characteristic humility taking the role of Pascal's lackey. When,
however, they were examined by the magistrates they admitted that they were Catholic. 'Of that we marvel,' was
the reply, 'for your Queen and all her realm are of our
religion.' But no difficulty was made of their admission, and
they were led to an inn where, with the genius of the race,
they were made exceptionally comfortable.

So far from being subdued by the kindness of their reception or the delicacy of their position in a hostile town, six

of the younger members, Campion and Persons among them, set out after dinner in a mood of exuberant high spirits to interview Theodore Beza, the prominent Calvinist, who at the moment enjoyed an international reputation as a theologian, greater, perhaps, in England than anywhere else. He was then an old man; in early life his ambitions had been purely literary, and he had earned considerable popularity in the composition of lubricious verse; later, falling in with Calvin and being disposed to settle down, he had married one of his mistresses, the wife of a Parisian tailor, and was now one of the nine elders of the Church of Geneva. His lady, Candida by name, opened the door and admitted them to the courtyard, where the old scholar came to see them, a venerable figure with long beard, dressed in black gown and skull cap, with a starched white ruff at the neck. The magistrates had told him of their arrival, and after an exchange of compliments he expressed his regret that they were not of the religion of their country.

Persons, who presumably understood the injunction they had received 'to avoid all sarcasm and prefer solid to sharp answers', as applying only to their behaviour in England, proceeded by a series of questions to show that, since the Calvinists admitted no inequality in ministry and governed their Church theocratically, while Elizabeth had appointed bishops and usurped for herself the entire jurisdiction of the Pope, the English Protestants were heretical even by his own standards.

The ground of the discussion then shifted, and Beza recounted a number of stories, which subsequently proved to be false, about the iniquities of the Duke of Guise; but

Campion, standing impatiently by in his servant's livery, could retain himself no longer and insisted on bringing the subject back to essentials, offering to demonstrate numerous features of the Elizabethan Church that were out of accordance with Beza's views. But Beza was not in the mood to waste an afternoon in his courtyard being catechized by a servant on questions of which there was little hope of agreement, so he called his wife to bring him another packet of letters, and took leave of the Fathers with remarkable courtesy of manner, promising to send them an English pupil of his, the son of Sir George Hastings, next-of-kin to the Earl of Huntingdon, who had greater leisure than himself for such discussions.

Hastings never arrived, but in his place there came to visit them at their inn a Mr. Brown and a Mr. Powell, two keen Anglicans, with whom the priests struck up a relationship of some cordiality, arguing well into the night, promenading the streets, breakfasting together, and eventually enjoying their company for the first mile or two of the journey north.

It was by Mr. Powell's advice that Persons was dissuaded from challenging Beza to a public disputation, the loser of which should be publicly burned alive in the market place. Thanks to him they left Geneva without embroiling themselves with the authorities, but could not be restrained from baiting an unfortunate clergyman whom they encountered, placidly conning a sermon, a mile out of the town. Campion and Fr. Bruscoe were ahead, and without introduction accosted the man and tackled him on the subject of Church government; at first he took them for sympathetic inquirers, but was speedily tied up on the question they had put to

Beza of Elizabeth's ecclesiastical supremacy; he turned for support in his confusion to the rest of the party, who fell upon him with relish, contradicted him, tripped him up in his arguments, and left him breathless with indignation, his fingers vainly fluttering the pages of his sermon, while Mr. Powell attempted to excuse the eccentricities of the strange company in which he had been found.

At the summit of a hill overlooking the city, the pilgrims paused and sang a *Te Deum* in acknowledgement of the enjoyable time they had spent there; and then, perhaps slightly in doubt of whether they had behaved with complete politeness, went out of their way over rough ground to do penance at the shrine of St. Claude, a place which, until its destruction during the French Revolution, was a great centre of devotion in that part of the country. From there they continued the journey in buoyant spirits and, until near the end, excellent health, to Rheims, where they arrived on the last day of May, having spent about six weeks on the way from Rome.

While they were on the road it was Campion's practice to say his Mass very early, and then, after reciting the *Itinerarium* with the others, to push on ahead for a few hours' solitary devotion, reading his breviary, reciting the Litanies of the Saints and telling his beads. When this was over he would allow the rest to overtake him, and would spend the day laughing and talking until evening, when he would again slip away from them for his meditation and prayers. One of his particular jokes, in which they all shared, was the terror with which they looked towards England and the probability of a painful death.

When they reached Rheims and caught up with Bishop Goldwell and Dr. Morton, they found that what had been fun to them had become a very grave matter to the Prelate. He was in his eightieth year and far from hardy; all his life he had been accustomed to soft living and deferential treatment. It had seemed easy enough during the wave of enthusiasm at Rome to volunteer for the expedition; he had left in an atmosphere of personal popularity which was novel and entirely agreeable to him; but the weeks of jogging along through water-logged high roads, of putting up at inns where the accommodation seemed totally inadequate for a person of his dignity, of not being recognized, of getting wet and having nothing dry to change into, above all of reflecting as he lay sleepless on the wholly unsuitable beds which he was obliged to occupy, that each day's painful journey was taking him farther from the life which he understood and nearer to those sufferings which had sounded so edifying when read aloud in the refectory, had effected a serious derangement of the bishop's system. At Rheims they received him with the utmost kindness; they were continually kissing his ring; but when they sought to be most complimentary they would applaud his courage by recounting with something very like relish the appalling severity of the new penal laws on the other side of the Channel. After a few days of it he took to his bed and began writing to the Pope to express his doubts whether he were precisely the best person for the work in hand. He had already written from Bologna, saying it had come to his ears that the Bishop of Lincoln was now out of prison; was there any object in his going on? The answer conveyed to him by the nuncio in Paris was sharp; that even if the rumour were true, there was room in England for two bishops. Now he wrote twice, mentioning his willingness to go anywhere and endure anything at His Holiness's command, but suggesting an alternative plan; why should not one or two of these courageous young priests be made bishops? It was not a question of money; they would be content to live in the poverty of the primitive Church.

To make matters worse, before there was time for a reply, plague broke out in Rheims, and the Bishop's agitation became frantic. Accordingly he settled matters for himself and returned to Rome without permission, where he was greeted by a somewhat cold reception from the Cardinal of Como. Dr. Allen allowed himself no recriminations, merely remarking that 'it was better the old man should yield to fear now than later on, on the other side'.

The other, more disturbing, piece of information which greeted the pilgrims at Rheims was that, at about the same time as their departure from Rome, Dr. Nicholas Sander had been dispatched as Papal nuncio, with five ships of men and arms, to assist the Geraldine rising in Ireland. The prudence of this step was more in doubt than the strict legality, for Ireland stood in a very different relation to the Holy See from that of England and Wales. Although it had once, in extremity, been admitted by King John, the Pope's feudal jurisdiction over England had been constantly and resolutely denied. Ireland, however, was, in feudal law, unquestionably a Papal fief, and had always been recognized as such by the English monarchy; moreover, it had never been effectively conquered or administered; outside the Pale English control had been negligible. The Pope had a legal right of interference, such as Elizabeth never enjoyed in the Netherlands, but to Campion, whose acquaintance with the country derived entirely from official circles in Dublin, the expedition seemed a shocking alliance with anarchy against the decent order of English jurisdiction, while to all the priests it was clear that Cecil's policy of identifying their cause with political treason would be greatly facilitated.

They learned moreover that Walsingham's agents had provided him with very complete descriptions of all the party, and that the Channel ports were being closely watched for their arrival.

How little this intelligence depressed the optimism of the party may be judged by the fact that before they had been more than a few days at Rheims the defection of Bishop Goldwell and Dr. Morton had been made up by two volunteers from the College, Dr. Ely and Father John Hart, and by Father Thomas Cottam, an invalid, who had been obliged by ill health to leave the Jesuit noviciate.

Campion as usual was called upon to preach; he did so, and the sermon is notable as being the first time for many years that he had spoken in public in his native language. Dr. Allen waited the issue with some anxiety, but any difficulties he may have expected were completely overcome, and Campion spoke as fluently and correctly as though he had never left England. The text which he chose was *Ignem veni mittere in terram*; once more employing the fire motive which appears frequently in his utterances, from his second debate before Elizabeth, through his letters to the novices at Brunn, to this memorable occasion when he cried the word so loudly that, Bombinus records, passers-by in the street took alarm and hastened to the water buckets.

He had long conversations with Dr. Allen in which it was clear that neither of them expected to meet again. 'As for me,' said Campion, 'all is over . . . I have made a free oblation of myself to His Divine Majesty, both for life and death, and I hope He will give me grace and force to perform; and this is all I desire.'

In this mood the missionaries separated to make their way, as best they could, in pairs and small companies, across the Channel. Dr. Brombury and Father Bruscoe went to Dieppe, Sherwin and Pascal to Rouen, Gilbert, Crane and Kemp to Boulogne, Ely, Rishton, Kirby, Hart and Cottam to Dunkirk. Persons, Campion and the lay brother Emerson went to the Jesuit house at St. Omer. There were several English fugitives there; they and the Flemish Fathers attempted to discourage the crossing, saying that the vigilance at Dover was now so great that their immediate arrest was inevitable, but Mr. George Chamberlain, a man of some consequence, was more hopeful and, since it was clear that whatever dangers awaited them would tend to become more, rather than less, grave with delay, Persons decided on immediate action. Disguised as a soldier with buff and gold braid and a soldierly, swaggering manner, Persons set out from Calais commanding Campion and Emerson to wait, get what information they could at the quayside of their superior's fortune, and, if all had turned out well, follow without delay.

For nine days they waited at St. Omer without news. Then a letter arrived, addressed by Persons to Campion in the capacity of jeweller, which he had decided to assume, urging him to come at once to London and market his wares. Accordingly Campion and Emerson set out, found a ship, and after four days in harbour waiting for a favourable wind, crossed on the evening of 24 June and landed at Dover before it was daylight.

PART III
THE HERO

THE HERO

In the nine years of Campion's absence from England William Cecil's position had become steadily stronger. He had been created Lord Burghley in 1571, and in the summer of the following year took the office of Lord Treasurer. He still kept control of the Star Chamber and of foreign affairs, while in 1574 he secured the appointment to his old position as Secretary of Sir Francis Walsingham, a man in absolute sympathy with himself in the aims and methods of Government. In 1572 Norfolk had gone to the scaffold; with him had died the hopes of the Conservative Party. Mary Stuart's cause had come to final ruin in Scotland with the surrender and death of Kirkcaldy and Maitland; she was a prisoner on English soil, and Cecil knew that with tact and patience he would, one day, persuade his mistress to order her execution. The Queen increased daily in popularity, particularly in London, the home counties and the ports, where she was accorded something nearly approaching divine honours. Cecil had her complete confidence. The Dudley circle, where it was now fashionable to be anti-French and Calvinist, might regard him with distrust, but the Queen drew a fairly clear distinction between the company with whom she amused herself and those whom she allowed to manage the affairs of State.

On the other hand, in foreign politics Cecil had not been

so successful. He had not foreseen the massacre of St. Bartholomew's Day, 1572, which had broken the supremacy of the Huguenots; deprived of French help, the insurgents in the Spanish Netherlands were being reconquered, and he had counted upon them to distract Spanish attention from the unremitting provocation offered by the English buccaneers. A Spanish war was to the interest of neither country. So far from being, as he appeared to many of Campion's contemporaries, the Catholic Ghengis Khan, sweeping irresistibly over Europe, Philip, we now know, was an intensely conscientious and far from competent bureaucrat, whom vast inherited dominions kept constantly embarrassed. No one knew better than himself the weakness that lay behind the elaborate façade of the Spanish monarchy; how vital dispatches got delayed and lost in the huge secretarial system of the Escurial; how revenues melted away as they passed from hand to hand between their source and the Treasury; how officials in his remote territories wilfully misconstrued their orders; how posts requiring the highest abilities were distributed by titles of birth; how priests were continually interfering and admonishing about his responsibilities and destinies, how his own stiff conscience was always prompting him into courses radically opposed to common sense, how the salaries and pensions were in arrears, troops mutinying for lack of pay, and pious foundations petitioning for subsidies which he could not find heart to refuse. The last thing he wanted was to go to war, particularly with the English, whose formidable spirit he knew from the days when he had been their king.

But the provocation had been continuous, from the

earliest days when Cecil had sent Dr. Man as ambassador, a person of atrocious manners who had referred to the Pope in front of half the Court as 'a canting little monk'. Then there had been the treasure which he had unloaded at Plymouth and Southampton, to convey under Elizabeth's safe conduct for re-embarkation at Dover. She had rescinded the safe conduct and commandeered the entire booty. Then there were the slave traders. In accordance with his stern moral code Philip forbade his American colonists from enslaving the native Indians and from importing negroes. They resented this, and readily bought from Hawkins, although trade of any kind was forbidden them except with their Mother Country. Not only was Elizabeth cognizant of this contraband business, she was a partner in it. She had lent a ship of her own, unsuitably called the *Jesus,* for this very purpose. Bristol grew rich once more with the trade that St. Wulstan had suppressed there in the eleventh century. English galleys, laden with human cargo, plied regularly between America and West Africa, and on their return journeys, as often as not, stopped to sack a Spanish outpost or board a treasure ship.

At this very time, the summer of the Jesuits' arrival, Drake was coming into home waters after three years of sensational good fortune in the Indies; Cecil had done all in his power to discourage the expedition, even to insinuating an agent of his own into the crew with instructions to raise a mutiny and conjure unfavourable winds, but the man had been detected and hanged from the yard-arm, and Drake's arrival with a hold full of plunder was acclaimed as a national triumph by the Queen herself. At present Philip was occupied in Portugal, where the English as usual had been intriguing with the pretender; when that was settled he would have to turn his mind to a punitive expedition.

There were numerous disturbing portents recorded on the even of the Jesuits' arrival. In April the great bell of Westminster tolled of itself without human agency. In June there were thunderstorms of exceptional violence. A woman named Alice Perin, at the age of eighty years, gave birth to a prodigy with a head like a helmet, a face like a man, a mouth like a mouse, a human body, eight legs, all different, and a tail half a yard long, while in the same year another monster was reported from Stowe that was both male and female, with mouth and eyes like a lion. In May a pack of hounds was clearly visible hunting in the clouds over Wiltshire, while over the border in Somerset three several companies of sixty men each, dressed in black, marched in procession through the sky. Cecil, Elizabeth and most of the Court took serious notice of auguries and the events caused great anxiety for the Government's security.

There was also the question of the Queen's projected marriage with the Duke of Anjou. In a general way, so long as Mary Stuart remained alive, everyone wished to see the Queen married, but the objections to every suitor, royal or common, seemed insuperable. For some years now, Castlenau, the French Ambassador, had been pressing forward the claims of the French prince. A personable agent, Simier, had been wooing her assiduously, and with some response. Elizabeth had already been warned that the Duke was not physically prepossessing, but his appearance, when finally he arrived, in the summer of 1578, startled the court. He was dwarfish in stature, with bandy legs, an enormous cleft nose and a profusion of pock marks. He was sexually perverted, and twenty years the Queen's junior. Contrary to all expectation she was enchanted with him, played with him by the hour, fondled him, and called him 'her little frog'. They formed a macabre pair, for Elizabeth was now in middle age, her face was shrunken, revealing the large, masculine bones beneath it, she was extravagantly painted and dressed, while over all towered a crimson wig, stuck with jewellery, which, it was reputed, covered a head that was totally bald. The flirtation, however, was carried to extremes of demonstration, and the general opinion held that at last the Queen's capricious heart was finally won. But the difficulty, as with so many of her suitors, lay in the question of their faith. The Duke's mother, Catherine of Medici, was impatient of religious scruples, but the little fellow held out for his Mass, and negotiations were protracted until, four years later, the project was at last abandoned. Meanwhile, however, in the year with which we are dealing, the Catholics watched the affair with tragic eagerness, for it was in that grotesque alliance that they saw the single, frail hope of their own survival.

It is still generally believed in England that Elizabeth's anti-Catholic legislation was remarkable for its leniency, and that in an age of savage intolerance she and Cecil stood out as unique examples of enlightenment and moderation. It may, therefore, be convenient to approach the English Catholics by means of a summary of their legal position.

Some of these measures have been mentioned above. By the two Acts of Supremacy and Uniformity which established the Church of England, there was imposed a fine of one shilling for non-attendance at the parish church, the proceeds of which were to go to the poor of the parish. It was also made illegal to hold any service, except those contained in the Prayer Book. An oath of submission to the Queen's spiritual supremacy was formulated, which might be tendered to all officials and to anyone found attending an illegal service. The penalty for a second refusal of this oath was death.

A later ordinance provided that anyone engaged in education, either as a schoolmaster or as a private tutor, must receive a licence from the Bishop of the diocese. A passport system at first hindered, and later prohibited, parents from sending their children to school abroad.

This was the situation up till 1570, the date of the Bull of Excommunication. It was then made high treason (punishable, of course, with death) to bring into the country 'any bull, writing or instrument obtained from the Bishop of Rome', 'to absolve or reconcile' any of the Queen's subjects, or to be absolved or reconciled. To bring into the country or receive any object of devotion, 'tokens, crosses, pictures, beads or such like vain things from the Bishop of Rome', was punishable by the confiscation of property.

In 1581, to meet the emergency of Campion's mission, a further Act was passed 'To retain the Queen Majesty's subjects in due obedience'. It reaffirmed the principle that it was high treason to reconcile anyone or to be reconciled to the Church and imposed a new scale of fines. For hearing Mass the penalty was 100 marks (£66 13s. 4d.) and a year's imprisonment.

This clause is notable because it is the first time that the Mass is specifically proscribed. Hitherto the offence had been 'to sing or say any common or open prayer or to minister any sacrament otherwise than is mentioned in the said book' (the Elizabethan Prayer Book). The same Act provides that the penalty for not attending church shall be £20 per month, per head, for those over sixteen years of age.

The object of this legislation was to outlaw and ruin the Catholic community. It will be seen that under the new code a family of four adults who elected to lead a regular Catholic life, attending Mass on days of obligation and eschewing the Protestant services, were liable, if they were fortunate enough to keep out of prison, to a total yearly payment of over £15,500 (or in modern currency about £93,000). This sum was to be divided into three parts, one of which went to the Treasury, one to the informer, and one to the poor of the parish, but there is no single instance on record of this last humane provision having been put into effect. There was scarcely an estate in the country capable of sustaining an imposition of this size, nor, in fact, was any obliged to do so, for the Masses were said in secret, the vessels kept behind sliding panels, and the priests smuggled in and out of doors through concealed passages, but one infraction of the code could not in its nature be kept hidden —the refusal to attend Protestant services—and from 1580 onwards the enormous tax of £240 (about £1,440 modern value) yearly for each adult member of a Catholic household was pretty regularly exacted; none but the wealthiest had any choice between submission and destitution.

The other penalties could not be enforced consistently. Some recusants were continually in and out of prison, some were left undisturbed for years together. The system was full of incongruities, such as Mass being regularly said in Marshalsea prison. Some provisions, such as that any man might be convicted of high treason who twice refused the Oath of Supremacy, seem never to have been put into force. Raids for proscribed objects—rosaries, religious pictures, crucifixes, etc.—took place capriciously. First one district would be combed out and then another. Everything depended on local goodwill and the activity of the professional informers.

Of these the best known and most successful was Richard Topcliffe, who first appears in history in 1578. From then onwards he was in regular employment under the Government hunting out Catholics. To him was accorded the privilege unique in the law of England, or, perhaps, of any country, of maintaining a private rack in his own house for the more convenient examination of prisoners. Only once did he fall into discredit, towards the end of his public life, in 1594, when he was brought to court by a colleague, Thomas Fitzherbert. 'For whereas Fitzherbert entered into bonds to give £5,000 unto Topcliffe, if he would persecute his father and his uncle unto death together with Mr. Bassett [from whom he expected legacies], Fitzherbert pleaded that the conditions were not fulfilled because they died naturally and Bassett was in full prosperity.' Evidence was given by Mr. Bassett himself that Topcliffe had done everything in human power to entrap him, and Coke, the Queen's attorney, confirmed him, testifying that Topcliffe had assiduously accused all three of Popery, but the court held that Topcliffe, for once, had been remiss in his duty and sentenced him to a short term in prison, of the injustice of which he complained bitterly, saying that it was enough to make the bones of Father Southwell dance for joy.

He and others like him now proceeded about the country levying blackmail where they could, spying, bribing servants, corrupting children, compassing the death of many innocent priests and the ruin of countless gentle families.

The Catholics were defenceless at law, for their whole inherited scheme of life had been dubbed criminal; they lived in day-to-day uncertainty whether they might not suddenly be singled out for persecution, their estates confiscated, their families dispersed and themselves taken to prison or the scaffold. Three examples of the manner in which the law was enforced even in the milder days before the coming of the Jesuits may be taken from the accounts of Elizabeth's progress through Norfolk in 1578.

The county was particularly strong in Catholics and they welcomed the opportunity to show their loyalty to the Queen. At Euston Hall, near Thetford, lived Edward Rookwood, a Catholic squire in the early twenties, newly married. Although there were many more magnificent houses in the neighbourhood, the Queen chose to come out of her way to stay at Euston. The house was ill-equipped for the accommodation of her large retinue, but the young couple exerted themselves to the utmost and, until the last morning, were hopeful that the visit had proved a success. When, however, Rookwood presented himself to kiss his guest's hand, he was roughly told to stand aside, was rated for being a Catholic, put under arrest and marched away to Norwich jail.

At first his Norfolk neighbours were inclined to attribute Rookwood's disgrace to the simplicity of his entertainment, but four days later the Queen crossed into their county to visit the former Lady Elizabeth Style, now married to Thomas Townshend of Braconash. Townshend had taken the oath of spiritual supremacy, but was related to several recusants and was on friendly terms with others. He lived in baronial splendour and the Court were here treated with the extravagance they expected, but the Queen took the opportunity of a party to have nine of her fellow-guests arrested under her host's roof and sent, like Rookwood, to Norwich, where the Court followed shortly.

About a mile from the city a gentleman named Downes rode out to meet them. He was a Catholic of ancient family, lord of the manor of Erlham, which he held from the Crown by Petit Serjeantry or service of a pair of spurs. Mr. Downes presented the Queen with the spurs, fashioned in gold, and began to recite some complimentary verses of his own invention. He was curtly ordered to stand aside and follow the party into Norwich, where he was clapped into prison.

These were the conditions of life, always vexatious, often utterly disastrous, of the people to whom the Jesuits were being sent, people drawn from the most responsible and honourable class, guilty of no crime except adherence to the traditional faith of their country. They were conditions which, in the natural course, could only produce despair, and it depended upon their individual temperaments

whether, in desperation, they had recourse to apostasy or
conspiracy. It was the work of the missionaries, and most
particularly of Campion, to present by their own example
a third, supernatural solution. They came with gaiety
among a people where hope was dead. The past held
only regret, and the future apprehension; they brought with
them, besides their priestly dignity and the ancient and
indestructible creed, an entirely new spirit of which Campion is the type; the chivalry of Lepanto and the poetry of
La Mancha, light, tender, generous and ardent. After him
there still were apostates and there were conspirators; there
were still bitter old reactionaries, brooding alone in their
impoverished manors over the injustice they had suffered,
grumbling at the Queen's plebeian advisers, observing the
forms of the old Church in protest against the crazy, fashionable Calvinism; these survived, sterile and lonely, for theirs
was not the temper of Campion's generation who—not the
fine flower only, but the root and stem of English Catholicism—surrendered themselves to their destiny without cal-
culation or reserve; for whom the honourable pleasures and
occupations of an earlier age were forbidden; whose choice
lay between the ordered, respectable life of their ancestors
and the faith which had sanctified it; who followed holiness,
though it led them through bitter ways to poverty, disgrace,
exile, imprisonment and death; who followed it gaily.

Campion's first action on landing on English soil was to
retire out of sight of the men, fall on his knees and commend
his cause to God; then as dawn was breaking he and Brother
Ralph went to interview the 'searcher', whose business it

was to inspect all immigrants. Persons, as they learned later, had got through with his usual adroitness, not only unsuspected by the officials, but on terms of easy cordiality with them. Campion was less successful; there had been a warning to watch the ports for the arrival of Gabriel Allen, Dr. Allen's brother, who was reported to be on his way to visit his family at Rossall. Campion and Ralph were therefore brought before the Mayor of Dover and interrogated; at first he seemed disposed to send them under guard to London, but unexpectedly changed his opinion and allowed them to go in freedom. They travelled by boat up the river to Hythe, in some doubt as to what their procedure should be on arrival in London; but Persons had arranged everything, and, as soon as they were moored to the quay, a man stepped on board, greeted Campion as 'Mr. Edmunds' and led them immediately to a house in Chancery Lane where Mr. George Gilbert had lodgings.

This was probably Campion's first meeting with Gilbert, but he was well known to him by repute. He was a wealthy layman, aged at this time twenty-eight, whose large properties in different parts of the country had been preserved and augmented during his long minority. He had been educated at London and Cambridge in strict Calvinist principles, being at one time particularly under the influence of Dr. Edward Dering, a prominent Anglican divine. At his coming of age he was handed over the unrestricted use of his fortune and sent abroad for the completion of his education. He was a good athlete, horseman and fencer, and his interests seem to have been mainly sporting until, at Paris, he came into contact with Father Thomas Darbyshire, who converted him to Catholicism. He went to Rome, where he put himself under the direction of Persons, and rapidly became absorbed in his new religion. He wished to make a pilgrimage to the Holy Land, but Persons deflected his enthusiasm to England, where he now returned and made himself the centre of a group of Catholic laymen of his own kind. They took into their pay the London pursuivants and were able to meet and hear Mass freely; the house in Chancery Lane where he was now living belonged to Adam Squire, the chief pursuivant and son-in-law of the Bishop of London. He was on the point of marrying an heiress at the time of the Fathers' arrival, but now took a vow of chastity until England should publicly return to the Faith. One of the blessings with which Pope Gregory had charged the Fathers was to this association of laymen, who were bound together by a vow to devote themselves to furthering the Church's progress, but do not appear to have constituted a sodality of the kind which was becoming common under Jesuit missions.

Persons was away in the country at the time of Campion's arrival and had left word for him to await his return. During these eight or ten days Campion made the acquaintance of most of the chief Catholics and Catholic sympathizers in London. On the Feast of St. Peter and St. Paul, 29 June, he preached on the historic text *Tu es Petrus* before a large audience in the hall of Lord Norrey's house, hired for the occasion by Lord Paget, and daily interviewed a great number who came to him for advice. There seems to have been a friend or agent at Court, for he was successfully protected from the informers who attempted to get access to him in the guise of penitents, among the most dangerous of whom was one Sledd, who had been a servant in Rome and knew by sight many of the missionaries. Persons and Campion had two narrow escapes from this man, in one of which Father Robert Johnson, a Marian priest, was taken and later executed. It had become clear that the Fathers could not remain hidden for long in London, and on Persons' return he set about preparations for their work in the country.

But first it was necessary to define the aims of the mission to the existing clergy and to discuss various topics of importance with the leading Catholics. Accordingly a conference, which has later been dignified with the name of the Synod of Southwark, was called in the second week of July at a small house on the south side of the river near St. Mary Overies. There were three or four Marian priests still at large in London, ministering in secret to the Catholic community; these—the names and exact number are not known —assembled under Father George Blackwell, the future Archpriest, with several of the seminary priests who had arrived in safety, and some of the laity—a combination which old-fashioned professional churchmen, such as Bishop Goldwell, might have regarded askance.

The questions debated were typical of the situation which confronted the missionaries. Persons was in charge of the proceedings. He first read to the meeting the instructions under which the missionaries were working, emphasizing the prohibition of political action and declaring on oath his ignorance, until his arrival at Rheims, of Dr. Sanders's expedition in Ireland.

The next question was one of vital importance to the laymen: the rule governing their attendance at Protestant services. A committee of the Council of Trent had already given a decision, but there had been no official promulgation of it (except to individuals here and there by Dr. Sanders) and many had found it convenient to profess ignorance. They could plead, with some reason, that there was nothing specifically anti-Catholic in the Morning Prayer, which would secure them immunity from persecution; it consisted of the recital of a creed identical with their own, readings from the Scriptures, psalms and prayers mostly translated from Catholic sources. In a great number of places the newly appointed clergy had no authority to preach, but had to content themselves with homilies, exhorting their flocks to virtue in unexceptionable terms. But no compromise was allowed. By the very importance which the Government attached to it, attendance at the new service constituted an act of adherence to the Elizabethan Settlement; it was not merely *participicio in sacris*, but a formal admission of the spiritual supremacy of the State. Accordingly Persons pronounced an absolute prohibition which placed anyone observing the law outside the Catholic body, in the words, 'So public an act as is going to the church, where profession is made to impugn the truth and to deface, alienate and bring into hatred Christ's Catholic Church, is the highest iniquity that can be committed.'

If anyone had remained in doubt of the missionaries' innocence of political motive, this verdict should have reassured them. If the object in their secret coming and going from house to house had been conspiracy; if, as was said by their enemies, they were using the confessional to prepare a concerted insurrection in support of Spain, they would have instructed their followers to equivocate with 'mental reservations', to lie low, to attend the services, take the oaths, and then at the appointed signal fall upon their unsuspecting neighbours; nothing would have been more recklessly imprudent, or fatal to their purpose, than to make their adherents advertise themselves publicly to the authorities.

The next question was ecclesiastical. Up to the Reformation there were various slight differences of rite in different parts of the country, the Sarum Use being the predominant one. There were now no more Sarum books printed and the priests arriving from abroad were all trained in the Roman rite. The old English one, moreover, was considerably stricter in matters of fasting than that generally followed on the Continent. The missionaries were asked whether any rule was to be observed universally throughout the country. The decision was that nothing should be altered from the old customs, but that each district should retain its traditional observance.

There were various particular cases cited for discussion. Father Cottam had been arrested at Dover and sent to London in charge of a fellow-traveller. The fellow-traveller was his colleague, Dr. Humphrey Ely, who under the name of Haward had crossed the Channel several times before, was well known at the port, and had a friend in the town who entertained him in ignorance of his identity. Dr. Ely allowed Cottam to escape, but as a result had been arrested himself, and, with him, his host at Dover, who had gone surety for him. Father Cottam asked whether it was his duty to give himself up and release his sureties; after some uncertainty the Synod decided he might; he did so with great cheerfulness, was imprisoned, and later died on the scaffold.

There was also the case of Father Bosgrave, another Jesuit, who had joined the Society sixteen years before and had since been working in Poland, far out of touch with the course of events in England. Now, at his superiors' bidding, he returned to England, sent, by a singular irony, for the good of his health. He was arrested immediately he landed, and taken for examination to the Bishop of London, who asked him whether he would go to church. 'I know no cause to the contrary,' he replied, and did so, to the great pleasure of the Protestant clergy, who widely published the news of his recantation. The Synod had only time to express their shame at his action before it broke up. The Catholics all shunned him, and Father Bosgrave, who retained only an imperfect knowledge of English, wandered about lonely and bewildered. Eventually he met a Catholic relative who explained to him roundly the scandal which he was causing. Father Bosgrave was amazed, saying that on the Continent scruples of this kind were not understood, but that a Catholic might, from reasonable curiosity, frequent a Jewish synagogue or an Anabaptist meeting-house if he felt so disposed. As soon as it was made clear to him that the Protestants had been claiming him as an apostate, he was roused to action, and, saying that he would speedily clear up that misunderstanding, wrote a letter to the Bishop of London which had the effect of procuring his instant imprisonment. He was confined first in the Marshalsea and later in the Tower, from which he was moved only to his trial and condemnation for high treason, a sentence that was later commuted to banishment. He then returned to Poland and resumed his duties there, having benefited less by his prolonged stay in England than his superiors had hoped.

As the little Council was coming to an end of its work a proclamation was issued by the Government which gave promise of further severe steps against the Catholics. This was dated 15 July; it announced, without giving confirmation of them, that there were rumours abroad of a Catholic League organized by the Pope and the King of Spain against the realm, and warned all loyal subjects to be 'in good readiness, with their bodies and arms' while those 'who have any unnatural affections are charged not to irritate Her Majesty to use the rod or sword of justice against them, from which, of her own natural goodness, she has a long time abstained'. It was, in fact, the preface to the Act already quoted 'for retaining the Queen Majesty's subjects in their due obedience', which was passed early in the following spring. The existing law was everywhere more rigorously enforced. Recusants who had been let out of prison on surety were now re-arrested. Watson, the aged Bishop of Lincoln, and Feckenham, the Abbot of Westminster, together with several other deposed dignitaries of the old Church, who had been allowed from time to time a measure of uneasy liberty, were now taken to Wisbech Castle and entrusted to men very different from the easy-going and corruptible jailers of the Marshalsea; no visitors were allowed them; no books except the Bible; they were kept apart from each other except at mealtimes, when their conversation was limited to bare civilities; they were obliged to find the expenses not only of themselves but of an Anglican chaplain who harangued them regularly in their cells and whose visits were as unacceptable as that of the harlot who was, on one occasion, locked up among them, not with the kindly, if misguided, notion of relieving their depression, but in order to damage the reputations of these aged men with the charge of incontinence.

The common gaols were soon full, and in all parts of the country castles were appointed for the reception of recusants —Banbury, Tremingham, Kimbolton, Portchester, Devizes, Melbourne, Halton and Wigmore—and in their catalogues may be found many famous names which survive among the Catholic community today—Tichborne, Stoner, Arundel, Throckmorton and countless others.

In these circumstances the Fathers left London for the provinces. Gilbert equipped them magnificently, giving each a pair of horses, a servant, the clothes suitable to a travelling gentleman and the substantial sum of £60 in ready money. He himself accompanied Persons for the first stage of his journey, while Campion went with another of the association, Mr. Gervase Pierrepoint. All travelled together for the first day and spent the night at Hoxton, at that time a village outside the city, at the house of a Protestant, perhaps Sir William Catesby, whose wife was Catholic. They arrived at nightfall and were about to start out again next morning when they were met by Mr. Thomas Pounde, who had slipped prison and ridden after them. Pounde was a devout and intelligent man, of pronounced eccentricity. The circumstances of his religious conversion were remarkable. He had been born with wealth and powerful family connexions, and for the earlier part of his life lived modishly and extravagantly at Court; his particular delight was in amateur theatricals, for which the fashion of the reign gave him ample scope. On one occasion he performed an unusually intricate *pas seul* before the Queen; it made a success with her and she called for a repetition. He complied, but, this time, missed his footing and fell full length on the ball-room floor. The Queen was more than delighted, gave out one of her uproarious bursts of laughter, kicked him, and cried 'Arise, Sir Ox'. Pounde picked himself up, bowed, backed out among the laughing courtiers with the words *Sic transit gloria mundi,* and from that evening devoted himself entirely to a life of austere religious observance. Various attempts, friendly and penal, failed to draw him back to his former habits, and in 1574 he was put into prison, after which date he was seldom at liberty, except on rare occasions like the present one; his cell at the Marshalsea became a resort of Catholic society, and it was there, in fact, that Persons had, on his arrival in London, first got into touch with Gilbert and the other members of the association.

It is not clear how Pounde was able to get away from prison, perhaps by a trick or by bribery, but it is most probable that he was let out on parole, for the régime at the Marshalsea was notoriously lax, and cases are even recorded of priests being allowed to spend the entire day at liberty, returning in the evening to sleep.

He came with a very wise suggestion. The prisoners had

been discussing the Jesuits' mission and the probability sooner or later of their capture; they feared that they might be taken and summarily executed without having the chance to plead their true intentions; the Government would be able to give their own account, forge confessions of treason, and no one would be in a position to contradict them. Accordingly Pounde asked the Fathers to draw up a written statement of their aims, which he would keep by him and publish in case of emergency. Persons and Campion agreed, and, sitting down there and then, each composed his own apologia, which Pounde carried back with him to the Marshalsea.

Even now, after the passage of more than three centuries, when the battle is on another ground and against other enemies, it is impossible to read *Campion's Brag* without emotion. At that day, to the ruined men at the Marshalsea, who for years had heard no news except of failure and betrayal, no arguments except those of the Puritan chaplains, whose triumphant, derisive, substantially documented sermons they were often obliged to hear; men cut off from the vivid Catholic life of Douai and Rome, who followed a loyalty which they themselves could not explain, against not only the fashion and authority, but what seemed to be the massed scholarship and reason of their age—the letter was intoxicating. As has been said above, it was composed in great haste, when the saddle bags were already packed and the horses waiting to take Campion on his journey; he needed no time for reflection, for the matter had been ceaselessly in his thoughts since he left Prague; it is the work of half an hour.

To the Right Honourable Lords of Her Majestie's Privy Council, it begins:

> Right Honourable,
> Whereas I have come out of Germanie and Boëmeland, being sent by my Superiours, and adventured myself into this noble Realm, my dear Countrie, for the glorie of God and benefit of souls, I thought it like enough that, in this busie, watchful and suspicious worlde, I should either sooner or later be intercepted and stopped of my course. Wherefore, providing for all events, and uncertaine what may become of me, when God shall haply deliver my body into durance, I supposed it needful to put this writing in a readiness, desiring your good Lordships to give it yr reading, for to know my cause. This doing, I trust I shall ease you of some labour. For that which otherwise you must have sought for by practice of wit, I do now lay into your hands by plaine confession.

He proclaims that he is a priest and a Jesuit, sent under obedience to England, to preach the gospel, minister the Sacraments and instruct the simple:

> . . . in brief, to crie alarme spiritual against foul vice and proud ignorance, wherewith many my dear Countrymen are abused.
> I never had mind, and am strictly forbidden by our Father that sent me, to deal in any respect with matter of State or Policy of this realm, as things which appertain not to my vocation, and from which I do gladly restrain and sequester my thoughts.

He then states with extreme simplicity that the Catholic case is unanswerable. Up till then the issue had chiefly depended upon sentiment, anti-Spanish feeling on the one hand, loyalty to tradition on the other. He now makes the claim, which lies at the root of all Catholic apologetics, that the Faith is absolutely satisfactory to the mind, enlisting all knowledge and all reason in its cause; that it is completely compelling to any who give it an 'indifferent and quiet audience'. This was something which had been consistently denied to it by the Elizabethan Government; accordingly he now appeals for an hearing before the Privy Council, with regard to its effect on 'the common weal', before the doctors and masters of the universities for its theology, and before the judicature for its legality.

He concludes with a peroration, every sentence of which is aflame with his own fiery spirit:

> Many innocent hands are lifted up to heaven for you daily by those English students, whose posteritie shall never die, which beyond seas, gathering virtue and sufficient knowledge for the purpose, are determined never to give you over, but either to win you heaven, or to die upon your pikes. And touching our Societie, be it known to you that we have made a league—all the Jesuits in the world, whose succession and multitude must overreach all the practices of England—cheerfully to carry the cross you shall lay upon us, and never to despair your recovery, while we have a man left to enjoy your Tyburn, or to be racked with your torments, or consumed with your prisons. The expense

is reckoned, the enterprise is begun; it is of God, it cannot be withstood. So the faith was planted: so it must be restored.

If these my offers be refused, and my endeavours can take no place, and I, having run thousands of miles to do you good, shall be rewarded with rigour, I have no more to say but to recommend your case and mine to Almightie God, the Searcher of Hearts, who send us His grace, and set us at accord before the day of payment, to the end we may at last be friends in heaven, when all injuries shall be forgotten.

It was characteristic of the two priests that Persons sealed his paper, while Campion left his open. Pounde read it that evening at the Marshalsea. Perhaps he showed it to some of the other prisoners. The effect, at any rate, upon his own somewhat volatile nature was instantaneous. There and then he set about the composition of a challenge on his own account, modelled upon Campion's; in the first instance, a brief thesis giving three reasons why Scripture should not be taken as the sole grounds of faith, which he followed, shortly afterwards, with an appeal for a formal dispute before the Bishops and Council.

Throughout the summer the prisoners at the Marshalsea had been obliged to listen to occasional exhortations from visiting Anglican divines. Now, on 16 August, the Bishop of London detailed two clergymen, Mr. Tripp and Mr. Robert Crowley, to act as regular chaplains. Little is known of Mr. Tripp; Mr. Crowley was rapidly rising to prominence as a leading low-churchman; he was above the average of his fellows as a scholar and had attracted favourable notice by his detestation of his surplice, which he described as his 'conjuring garment'. Former missionaries had found their audience at the Marshalsea torpid and indisposed to argument. Mr. Tripp and Mr. Crowley met with lively opposition and, unwilling to miss any opportunity for pushing himself forward, Mr. Crowley set about a pamphlet in reply to Pounde's *Three Reasons*. But the Bishop of London had no desire to see the Marshalsea prison turned into a school of theological debate, and he quickly silenced Pounde by removing him to chains and solitary confinement in a cell in the half-ruined palace at Bishop's Stortford. In these circumstances, if not before, Pounde passed on the text of *Campion's Brag* to his fellow-prisoners. Copies were made and circulated rapidly from hand to hand; visitors to the Marshalsea carried them into the city and the countryside. They came to the notice of the Bishop of Winchester, the Sheriff of Wiltshire, and other Government men; whenever found they were destroyed and their possessors arrested, but the paper spread rapidly among friend and enemy. The document originally intended as a final vindication in case of Campion's arrest or summary execution thus became, as by its spirit and form was eminently suitable, the manifesto of his mission.

The result, both for good and ill, was a vast augmentation of Campion's fame. This, obscured now by his long absence abroad, had, even in the old days before his exile, been local and limited; he was known at the universities and at Court, among scholars, men of affairs and men of fashion, but it is improbable that his name had ever reached the market towns and remote manors, where now it became fabulous.

Both sides now looked upon him as the leader and spokes-man of the new mission; his membership of the Society of Jesus cast over him a peculiar glamour, for, it must be remembered, the Society had, so far, no place in the English tradition. Many Englishmen could remember the day when the great estates were religious property; when friars tramped the roads from village to village, and monks, ton-sured and habited, drove their animals to market and dis-pensed alms and hospitality to the destitute; many had had their earliest lessons from Dominican or Benedictine in the drowsy village schools; the desolate monuments of the old Orders stood in every county; their names were familiar and their memory still sweet with the gentleness and dignity of a lost age. But 'Jesuit' was a new word, alien and modern.

To the Protestant it meant conspiracy. The countryman knew for himself the virtues and defects of the old monks; he had seen the methods by which the Royal Commissioners obtained their evidence, and he understood their motives perfectly; but of the Jesuits he knew nothing, except dis-torted and monstrous reports; that their founder was a Spaniard and that they were sworn to another allegiance than the Queen's. Stories of Spanish atrocities were eagerly devoured; the Jesuits were the vanguard of Spanish invasion; their business was to murder the Queen and the Council, and set the country in anarchy so that Philip could march in with the tortures of the Inquisition. Preposterous tales ob-tained credence of the Jesuits' rule and training and the enormous crimes daily committed behind their walls. The news that disguised Jesuits were now at large in the English countryside caused indignation and alarm, and those who had been apathetic in helping the authorities when the quarry was a Marian priest, now joined fiercely in the hunt.

To the Catholics, too, it meant something new, the restless, uncompromising zeal of the counter-Reformation. The Queen's Government had taken away from them the priest that their fathers had known; the simple, unambitious figure who had pottered about the parish, lived among his flock, christened them and married them and buried them; prayed for their souls and blessed their crops; whose attainments were to sacrifice and absolve and apply a few rule-of-thumb precepts of canon law; whose occasional lapses from virtue were expected and condoned; with whom they squabbled over their tithes, about whom they grumbled and gossiped; whom they consulted on every occasion; who had seemed, a generation back, something inalienable from the soil of England, as much a part of their lives as the succession of the seasons—he had been stolen from them, and in his place the Holy Father was sending them, in their dark hour, men of new light, equipped in every Continental art, armed against every fraility, bringing a new kind of intellect, new knowledge, new holiness. Campion and Persons found themselves travelling in a world that was already tremulous with expectation.

We have few details of this expedition. The two priests separated at Hoxton and met again three months later at Uxbridge; in the intervening time Persons had passed through Gloucester, Hereford, Worcester and up into Derbyshire; Campion had been in Berkshire, Oxfordshire and Northamptonshire. Both they and their hosts were careful to leave no record of their visits, and the letters in which the Jesuits reported progress to their superiors maintain strict anonymity for their converts; edifying anecdotes are related of 'a certain noble lady' who was offered her liberty on the condition of once walking through a Protestant church, but indignantly refused; of 'a young lady of sixteen' who was flung into the public prison for prostitutes on account of her courageous answers to the 'sham Bishop of London'; of a 'boy of, I believe, twelve years' who was inveigled into acting as page at a Protestant wedding, was inconsolable with shame until he was able to make his confession to a priest—but nothing is said to identify the protagonists. The only names that can be given with any certainty as Campion's hosts during this journey are Sir William Catesby of Ashby St. Leger, Lord Vaux of Harrowden and Sir Thomas Tresham, a man of exceptional character, eventually brought to ruin for his faith, whose singular and brilliant taste in architecture may still be seen in the exquisite, unfinished mansion at Lyveden and the unique, triangular pavilion, planned and intricately decorated in honour of the Trinity, which stands, concealed and forlorn, among the trees that border the park at Rushton. It is possible, however, to form a tolerably clear, general impression of the journey from the letters already mentioned and the numerous sources of information about Elizabethan conditions.

He travelled in fair comfort, mounted and equipped as befitted a gentleman of moderate means. He was attended by his servant, and more often than not by one or more of the younger members of the household where he had last stayed, but it was his habit for most of the way to ride in silence at some little distance from his companions, praying and meditating as he had done on the road to Rheims. Changes of horse and clothing were provided for him at different stages; he was constantly on the move, rarely, for fear of the pursuivants, stopping anywhere for more than one night. He must in this way have visited fifty or more houses during the three months.

Along his road the scenes were familiar enough, but he was seeing them with new eyes; the scars of the Tudor revolution were still fresh and livid; the great houses of the new ruling class were building, and in sharp contrast to their magnificence stood the empty homesteads of the yeomen, evicted to make way for the 'grey-faced sheep' or degraded to day-labour on what had once been their common land; the village churches were empty shells, their altars torn out and their ornaments defaced; while here and there throughout his journey he passed, as, with a different heart, he had often passed before, the buildings of the old monasteries, their roofs stripped of lead and their walls a quarry for the new contractors. The ruins were not yet picturesque; moss and ivy had barely begun their work, and age had not softened the stark lines of change. Many generations of orderly living, much gentle association, were needed before, under another Queen, the State Church should assume the venerable style of *Barchester Towers*. But if the emotions of the journey were shame and regret, hope and pride waited for him at the end of the day. Wherever they went the priests found an eager reception. Sometimes they stayed in houses where only a few were Catholic. There was constant coming and going in the vast, ramshackle households of the day, and an elaborate hierarchy in the great retinues; there were galleries where the master never penetrated. It was natural enough that any respectable wayfarer should put up there for the night, whether or not he had any acquaintance with his host.

> We passed through the most part of the shires of England [wrote Persons], preaching and administering the sacraments in almost every gentleman's and nobleman's house that we passed by, whether he was Catholic or not, provided he had any Catholics in his house to hear us. We entered for the most part, as acquaintance or kinsfolk of some person that lived within the house, and when that failed us, as passengers or friends of some gentleman that accompanied us; and after ordinary salutations we had our lodgings, by procurement of the Catholics, within the house, in some part retired from the rest, where putting ourselves in priests' apparel and furniture,

they heard confessions, perhaps preached, and very early next morning said Mass, gave communion and started on their way again, leaving the rest of the household in ignorance of their identity.

At Catholic houses they found themselves guests of the highest honour, and there they sometimes prolonged their stay for a few days, until the inevitable warning of the pursuivants' approach drove them once more on to the road. In recent years most of the houses had been furnished with secret cupboards where were stored the Mass vestments, altar stones, sacred vessels and books; these 'priest-

holes' were usually large enough to provide a hiding-place
for the missionaries in case of a sudden raid; in some cases
there were complete chapels with confessionals and priest's
room. Many houses sheltered one of the old Marian priests
who had left his cure at Elizabeth's succession, and now
lived in nominal employment as secretary and butler. At
this early date these seculars had no quarrel with the Fathers
of the Society. The Jesuits, fresh from Rome and the Continental schools, were as welcome to them as to their flocks;
cut off, as they were, from episcopal control, from their
reading and from intercourse with other clerics, they constantly found themselves confronted with problems to which
their simple training afforded no solution; all these were
brought to Campion and Persons. Their prayers were always
for more Jesuits.

> The priests of our country [wrote Campion], being
> themselves most excellent for virtue and learning, yet
> have raised so great an opinion of the Society, that I
> dare scarcely touch the exceeding reverence all
> Catholics do unto us. How much more is it requisite
> that such as hereafter are to be sent to supply, whereof
> we have great need, be such as may answer all mens
> expectation of them.

And Persons:

> It is absolutely necessary that more of our Society
> should be sent . . . who must be very learned men,
> on account of the many entangled cases of conscience,
> which arise from no one here having ample faculties,
> and from the difficulty of consulting the Holy See.

Campion found his Catholic hosts impoverished to the verge of ruin by the recusancy fines; often the household were in mourning for one or more of their number who had been removed to prison. 'No other talk but of death, flight, prison, or spoil of friends', yet everywhere he was amazed at the constancy and devotion which he found. The listless, yawning days were over, the half-hour's duty perfunctorily accorded on days of obligation. Catholics no longer chose their chaplain for his speed in saying Mass, or kept Boccaccio bound in the covers of their missals. Driven back to the life of the catacombs, the Church was recovering their temper. No one now complained of the length of the services, a priest reported to Father Agazzari: if a Mass did not last nearly an hour they were discontented, and if, as occasionally happened, several priests were together, the congregation would assist at five or six Masses in one morning.

Word would go round the countryside that Campion had arrived, and throughout the evening Catholics of every degree, squire and labourer and deposed cleric, would stealthily assemble. He would sit up half the night receiving each in turn, hearing their confessions and resolving their difficulties. Then before dawn a room would be prepared for Mass. Watches were set in case of alarm. The congregation knelt on the rush-strewn floor. Mass was said, communion was given. Then Campion would preach.

It needs little fancy to reconstruct the scene; the audience hushed and intent, every member of whom was risking liberty and fortune, perhaps his life, by attendance. The dusk lightened and the candles paled on the improvised altar, the tree tops outside the window took fire, as Campion spoke. The thrilling tones, the profusion of imagery, the polish and precision, the balanced, pointed argument, the whole structure and rich ornament of rhetoric which had stirred the lecture halls and collegiate chapels of Oxford and Douai, Rome, Prague and Rheims, inspired now with more than human artistry, rang through the summer dawn. And when the discourse had mounted to its peroration and the fiery voice had dropped to the quiet, traditional words of the blessing, a long silence while the priest disrobed and assumed once more his secular disguise; a hurried packing away of the altar furniture, a few words of leave taking, and then the horses' hooves clattered once more in the cobbled yard; Campion was on his way, and the Catholics dispersed to their homes.

The danger was increasingly great.

> I cannot long escape the hands of the heretics [said Campion, in the letter quoted above], the enemy have so many eyes, so many tongues, so many scouts and crafts. I am in apparel to myself very ridiculous; I often change my name also. I read letters sometimes myself that in the first front tell news that Campion is taken. . . . Threatening edicts come forth against us daily. . . . I find many neglecting their own security to have only care of my safety.

More than once while Campion was sitting at dinner strangers would be heard at the outer doors. 'Like deer when they hear the huntsmen' the company would leap to their feet and Campion would be rushed into hiding. Sometimes it proved to be a false alarm; sometimes the pursuivants would enter, question the inmates, and depart satisfied. The party would resume their meal and the interrupted conversation. Events of this kind were now a part of his life, but by the loyalty and discretion of his friends, and by his own resources, he escaped unmolested through the three-month journey, and his report ends in a triumphant mood:

> There will never want in England men that will have care of their own salvation, nor such as shall advance other men's; neither shall this Church here ever fail so long as priests and pastors shall be found for their sheep, rage man or devil never so much.

London was the centre of danger for the priests; the meeting of Campion and Persons was therefore brief. They reported progress, discussed plans, redistributed their resources, and parted again after the mutual confession and renewal of vows which was customary in the Society. There were other priests, seminarist and Marian, and probably several of their lay supporters at the Uxbridge meeting. The names have not been recorded. Father Hartley and Father Arthur Pitts were sent to the universities. (Both were caught later by the authorities. Father Hartley was hanged.) There was some discussion of a project towards Scotland, later put into effect by Father Holt, which has no part in Campion's story. His instructions were to proceed north to Lancashire, where many Catholic families were petitioning for his services, and if circumstances permitted, to produce a literary work, a Latin tract addressed primarily to the universities, which should follow up with solid argument the sensation made by the *Brag*. Persons remained in and about London. The search for him was incessant. A few weeks brought the news that Ralph Sherwin, most charming and devoted of the seminarists, had been taken, preaching in the house of a Mr. Roscarock. Bosgrave, Hart and Cottam were already in prison; Bruscoe was arrested on Christmas Eve. By constant changes of disguise and name and daring effrontery in his choice of residence, Persons succeeded in remaining at liberty; sometimes he attached himself to the Spanish Ambassador, sometimes he bribed the pursuivants and lodged with them, on one occasion at least he seems to have stayed in one of the royal palaces. All the time he pushed on the work with unremitting zeal. A great need of the Catholic party in the controversy which their activity had aroused was a printing press. The difficulties were formidable; every transaction, even the purchase of paper, was fraught with danger, and we shall see, when we come to examine Campion's *Ten Reasons,* how meagre the apparatus was, but a press of a kind he was able to procure, which he set up first at East Ham and later at Stonor Park, near Henley. The first production was an English composition of his own, the *Reasons Why Catholiques Refuse* to attend the Protestant services. There is no evidence that this work attracted much attention, but its successor was more sensational.

On 30 December and 3 January, respectively, there appeared pamphlets by two Anglican clergymen, Mr. Charke and Mr. Hanmer. Hanmer was a Welshman, who in 1567 had been chaplain of Christ Church at Oxford, and later became vicar of St. Leonard's church in London, where he tore up and sold the memorial brasses. He seems to have been a cheerful, bombastic person, free from malice, with small sympathy for his Puritan colleagues. 'A poor, dear soul,' Father Fitzsimon later described him, 'much given to banqueting and drinking and jesting and scoffing.'

Charke was a protégé of Burghley's, and a man of far stricter disposition. He had got into trouble at Cambridge for declaring the episcopal system to be the invention of Satan. At the disputations in the Tower he was later to prove one of Campion's most ill-mannered antagonists.

As might be expected, Charke's pamphlet was the more likely to prove damaging. It is entitled *An Answer to a Seditious Pamphlet lately cast about by a Jesuit,* and affords an instructive comparison both in style and matter with Campion's *Brag*. Briefly summarized, Charke's points are:

(1) The Church of Rome is the Church of Anti-Christ and her priests the priests of Anti-Christ, who take upon them 'against the manifest word of God to offer a sacrifice for the quick and the dead'. Campion had described himself as an 'unworthy' priest; 'to judge an evil servant by his own mouth, he, that is worthy of so foul a priesthood, what shall he be worthy of?'

(2) In old time the friars and monks used to name themselves Franciscans, Dominicans, etc., after 'base and beggarly friars'. Campion has the blasphemous presumption to take the name of Jesuit.

(3) They preach not the Gospel but against the Gospel . . . their ministry of the Sacraments is the saying or singing of mass and corrupt baptism.

(4) Religion and politics in England are, through God's

singular blessings, preserved together in life, as with one spirit; he that doth take away the life of the one, doth procure the death of the other. . . . Because he carrieth no sword he would be thought to carry no weapon. But is not the trumpet worse than many swords?

(5) Natural and moral reason, to which Campion appealed, are 'the two great enemies of true religion and the great nurseries of Atheism and Heresy'. Canon Law is 'ludicrous'.

(6) Campion speaks of 'innocent hands'. How can they be innocent when 'they crucify the Son of God again every day in their most blasphemous sacrifice of the Mass'?

This was the Anglican case which the Jesuits were called to meet. Except in its fourth section, it was not formidable, but the author must have felt confident that in the state of the censorship and the fugitive condition of his opponents, they would find it impossible to publish a reply. Within a week Persons had his answer written and printed. His *Censure* of Hanmer and Charke was adequate to the occasion, though it affords little interest to a modern reader. Even in its own day its chief importance was the fact of its appearance. It was suddenly brought home to the Government that there was in their midst an effective machinery working against their interests, that their pamphleteers could no longer pour out whatever abuse and misrepresentation they pleased without fear of correction. The speed of Persons' reply made it clear that he was on the spot; this was not one of the tracts emanating from the seminaries abroad. Their alarm found expression in the proclamation dated 10 January 1581, for 'recalling her Majesty's subjects which under pretence of studies do live beyond the seas both contrary to the laws of God and of the realm, and against such as do receive or retain Jesuits and massing priests, sowers of sedition and of other treasonable attempts'.

By this proclamation the relatives of seminarists had to recall them, or lose all civil rights. It was illegal to send them any supplies. Jesuits and priests must be surrendered; anyone knowingly harbouring them was guilty of sedition and treason.

The Jesuits were already outlaws, and as regards the legal position of them and their hosts the proclamation made little change, but its significance was that by forcibly reaffirming the existing law, the Council was giving warning of a further increase of severity in its application. Already, on 10 December, the Council had started in the case of Kirby and Cottam what was henceforth to be its consistent policy, of putting their religious prisoners to the torture. In the next four weeks, Sherwin, Johnson, Hart, Orton, Thomson and Roscarock were racked, Sherwin on two succeeding days. On 25 January Sir Walter Mildmay, in the House of Commons, rose to move the Bill for 'the retaining of Her Majesty's subjects in due obedience' quoted at the beginning of this chapter.

News of these events reached Campion in Lancashire and Yorkshire. About six months passed between the conference at Uxbridge and Campion's return to London. They were spent, as before, in visiting Catholic houses of whose names we have some fragmentary information. He spent Christmas with the Pierrepoints of Holme Pierrepoint; on the Tuesday after Twelfth-night he was in Derbyshire at Henry Sacheverell's, from whom he went to Mr. Langford, to Lady Foljambe of Walton, and to Mr. Powdrell, where he met George Gilbert, and perhaps received copies of Hanmer's and Charke's pamphlets. From there he visited Mr. Ayers of the Stipte. All this time he was under the conduct of Gervase Pierrepoint; in the third week of January Mr. Tempest took him in charge and led him into Yorkshire. On 28 January he was at Yeafford as the guest of Mr. John Rookby. In the succeeding weeks he visited Dr. Vavasour, Mrs. Bulmer, Sir William Bapthorpe of Osgodby, Mr. Grimston (probably Mr. Ralph Grimston of Nidd, who was hanged seventeen years later for harbouring Father Snow), Mr. Hawkeworth and Mr. Askulph Cleesby. Tempest was then succeeded by a Mr. Smyth, who took him to his brother-in-law's, Mr. William Harrington of Mount St. John, where Campion made a stay of twelve days, and so impressed William, one of his host's six sons, that he became a priest, and was later hanged. From Mount St. John he travelled with a Mr. More and his wife into Lancashire, where almost the whole county was Catholic in sympathy. Here he stayed with the Worthingtons, Talbots, Heskeths, Mrs. Allen, widowed sister-in-law of the Cardinal, Houghtons, Westbys and Rigmaidens. In the middle of May he was summoned to return to London.

These names are taken from Burghley's list, drawn up after Campion's arrest. It is far from complete, as will appear later from his letter to Lord Huntingdon. Probably twice its number remained undetected, if, as it is reasonable to suppose, Campion maintained the practice of constant change of residence. It is significant that much of Burghley's information seems to be of places where Campion remained some days and thus risked attracting the attention of Protestant informers; other names, such as Sir William Bapthorpe's and Dr. Vavasour's, were already well known to the authorities; Vavasour had been in prison at Hull in the preceding August, and Bapthorpe had given a bond of £200 to the Archbishop for his good behaviour.

His work in the north was apostolic, as it had been in the Midlands. Nearly a century later Father Henry More found that the tradition of Campion's passage was still fresh in Lancashire, and that Catholics still spoke of his sermons on the Hail Mary, the Ten Lepers, the King who went on a journey, and the Last Judgement. Perhaps he was more free in his movements, as danger lost its novelty; he seems to have preached more openly and to larger audiences than he had dared do during his first journey.

Besides this he was employed in writing the *Ten Reasons*. As we have noticed, the project was discussed at Uxbridge. Various suggestions had been made for its title, until Campion had proposed *De Haeresi Desperata*—'Heresy in Despair'; it was a suggestion typical of the spirit of the missionaries; on every side heresy seemed to be triumphant; the Queen's Government was securely in power; the old Church was scattered and broken; they themselves were being hunted from house to house in daily expectation of death; their very existence was a challenge to the power of the State to destroy a living Faith. Leading Catholics, such as Francis Throckmorton, were discussing a treaty with the Government in which they proposed to compound their fines for a regular subsidy on condition of being allowed the quiet practice of their religion. All despaired of the restoration of the Church, and only begged sufferance to die with the aid of her sacraments. It was at this juncture that Campion gently proposed to examine the despair of heresy and show that all its violence sprang from its consciousness of failure.

It is not certain why he changed his mind. Perhaps he felt that the issues were too grave for a display of high spirits; Charke, Hanmer and other Anglican critics had made great play with his 'insolence' in taking upon himself, in the *Brag*, to challenge the combined scholarship of his country; it was necessary to show that his confidence was founded on the strength of his case, not of his own skill. Whatever the reason, the book, when it appeared, bore the title *Decem Rationes*, 'Ten Reasons, for the confidence with which Edmund Campion offered his adversaries to dispute on behalf of the Faith, set before the famous men of our Universities.' It was composed, for the most part, at Mount St. John, and the manuscripts was sent to Persons soon after Easter. It was primarily for the purpose of seeing it through the press that Campion was called back to London at Whitsun.

The difficulties of production were very great. The margins were copiously annotated with textual references, all of which would be scrutinized by his opponents; accuracy was of vital importance, for any slip would be eagerly advertised as evidence of dishonesty. A young convert,

Mr. Fitz-Herbert, who was so far unsuspected by the Government and was therefore able to work without embarrassment, undertook to verify the references, but both Campion and Persons were anxious that the author should have the final reading. Before the date of Campion's arrival in London, it had been found necessary to move the press from East Ham, for the search was closing in. In March, the servant of Roland Jenks, a stationer who helped supply Persons with materials, turned informer; Persons' lodgings were raided and most of his personal possessions seized; more serious still, Father Briant was arrested in a neighbouring house and taken to the Tower, where, after more than usually savage torture, he emerged only for his execution. Shortly afterwards, one of Persons' workmen was arrested while on an errand in London, and racked, without success, to make him reveal the hiding-place of the press. In these circumstances Persons removed to Henley, where Dame Cecilia Stonor, mother of the Sir Francis of the day, put her house at his disposal. It was well suited for the purpose, being hidden in woods and easily accessible by river from London and Oxford. Here the *Decem Rationes* was printed, under the supervision of Stephen Brinkley, who, with the four workmen, was subsequently arrested.

Only four copies of the first edition are known to exist; one is in the possession of the Marquess of Bute, another is exhibited in the library at Stonyhurst; a third was in the possession of a Canon of Windsor in 1914; a fourth was discovered in 1936 in the sixpenny-box of a second-hand bookshop and is now in Campion Hall library. At first sight the little volume—it is barely 20,000 words in length—

shows little evidence of the difficulties under which it was produced. It has an elegantly spaced title page, decorated with a sacred emblem; the press-work is regular and the composition free from misprints. An expert examination has revealed certain peculiarities. Since the work is in Latin, Roman type had been used (Persons' English tracts were in black letter), but the printers were working at the disadvantage of great poverty of materials; after the first pages the diphthong 'Æ', which occurs frequently, runs out, and is replaced by the italic '*Æ*', by 'E', and even by '*E*'. These substitutions become more frequent as we approach the end of signatures C, H and I, while at the beginning of the next signature the fount Æ reappears, suggesting that the sheets were printed off and the type distributed and reset three times during the printing. There is no Roman query sign; black letter is used in its place. There is no Greek fount; Campion's Greek quotations have to be given in Roman italics.

It is not surprising that, in these circumstances, the book took several weeks to print off, but it was ready in time for Commencement at Oxford, Tuesday 27 June. The distribution was made by Father Hartley, the priest mentioned above, who was in close association with Persons at this period. Copies were introduced into St. Mary's church and placed on the benches. Campion's name was still well remembered in Oxford. The polished Livian style of the essay and the romantic manner of its appearance made an appeal to the university, where repeated repressive measures had failed to destroy traces of the old Faith, and, from the first, it became the centre of controversy.

In the present century it is difficult to understand the

sensation which was aroused. The Church has vast boundaries to defend, and each generation finds itself called to service upon a different front. The apologetics of another century seem to be concerned with truisms and trivialities, and modern Catholics are unlikely to find much that is useful in the *Ten Reasons*. The thesis may be analysed as follows:

(1) All heretics have been obliged to mutilate Holy Scripture in their own interest. The Lutherans and Calvinists have done this in several instances. (2) In other cases they retain the text, but pervert the clear meaning of the passage. (3) The Protestants by denying the existence of a visible Church, deny, for all practical purpose, the existence of any Church. (4) The Protestants pretend to revere the first four General Councils, but deny many of their doctrines. (5) and (6) The Protestants are obliged to disregard the Fathers. (7) The History of the Church is continuous. The Protestants are without living tradition. (8) The works of Zwingli, Luther and Calvin contain many grossly offensive statements. (9) The Protestants are obliged to employ many empty tricks of argument. (10) The variety and extent of Catholic witness are impressive. This section contains the eloquent passage:

Listen, Elizabeth, most powerful Queen . . . I tell thee; one and the same heaven cannot hold Calvin and the Princes whom I have named [Elizabeth's ancestors, and the great heroes of Christendom]. With these Princes then associate thyself, and so make thee worthy of thy ancestors, worthy of thy genius, worthy of thy excellence in letters, worthy of thy praises, worthy of thy fortune. To this effect only do I labour about thy person, and will labour, whatever shall become of me, for whom these adversaries so often augur the gallows, as though I were an enemy of thy life. Hail, good Cross. There will come, Elizabeth, the day that will show thee clearly which have loved thee, the Society of Jesus or the offspring of Luther.

It was a work of its own day, and the measure of its quality was the effect which it had on Campion's contemporaries. Burghley took up the matter as one of gravity and instructed the Bishop of London to produce an answer; the Regius Professors of Divinity at both Oxford and Cambridge were enlisted, and before 1585 no fewer than twenty works had appeared, dealing either with the *Brag,* the *Ten Reasons,* or the Disputes in the Tower, which were their direct consequence. Catholic theologians, who are notoriously critical of each other's work, combined to praise it. It was commended by the Cardinal Secretary of State, and Marc Antoine Muret, who, after a dangerous youth, was now established in honour at Rome, and enjoyed international pre-eminence as a Catholic humanist, described it as '*Libellum aureum, vere digito Dei scriptum*'—'a golden little book, truly written by the finger of God'. Since his day it has been reprinted nearly fifty times.

We have no exact information of Campion's movements in the two months which he spent in and about London. He was certainly at Stonor for part of this time, revising the proofs of the *Ten Reasons*. He appears to have frequented three lodgings in London, Mrs. Brideman's in Westminster, Mr. Barnes' in Tothill Street, and Lady Babington's in the White Friars. He also visited the Bellamys at Uxender Hall, Harrow-on-the-Hill, and made a few expeditions into the Midlands, to the Prices at Huntingdon, Mr. William Griffith at Uxbridge, Mr. Edwin East of Bledlow, Bucks, Lady Babington at Twyford, Bucks, Mr. Dormer at Wynge, and a Mrs. Pollard. The hunt was working nearer to him. The raid on Persons' headquarters in Bridewell had seriously embarrassed the two Fathers. Since the new year there had been, as was mentioned above, a series of arrests in their immediate circle, and it was in a mood of resignation that Campion awaited the doom which, with the pitiless step of ancient tragedy, came daily closer to him. Persons records how, as this time, he and Campion sat up most of one night, reviewing their situation and speculating how they would acquit themselves when the ordeal came.

Persons was to live on; his destiny was to lead him through many by-ways; his work was to be multifarious, obscure, inconclusive; there were to be days of tumult and of impenetrable silence, ceaseless effort, partial victory, fame that was spread in doubtful accents. For Campion there was only glory; a name of triumph and pure light. But as the figure of Persons recedes from view down the gloomy corridor of the Escurial, it is Campion's rope that he wears, knotted about his waist.

With the publication of the *Ten Reasons* the first part of Campion's task was accomplished. He had been in England, now, for over a year; that was his achievement, that in all her centuries the English Church was to count one year of her life by his devotion; others were now ready to take over the guard; since Easter thirty of Allen's priests had crossed the Channel and landed successfully; the work would go on; Mass would still be offered in England, the growing generation would still learn the truths of the faith; the Church of Augustine and Edward and Thomas would still live; for Campion there remained only the final sacrifice. His road to Harrow took him past Tyburn gibbet, and here, Persons records, he would often pause, hat in hand, 'both because of the sign of the Cross and in honour of some martyres who had suffered there, and also because he used to say that he would have his combat there'.

On Tuesday 11 July Campion took his leave of Persons, intending to collect some papers which he had left at Mr. Houghton's house in Lancashire, and then proceed into Norfolk upon another round of visits. They made their mutual confessions and renewal of vows, and on parting exchanged hats—as, on leaving Prague, Campion had exchanged his gown with the Rector, Campanus—a gesture, perhaps, signifying a particular solemnity and finality in the occasion. But in a short time Campion was back, to ask his superior's permission to break his journey at a house which lay almost directly on his route, Lyford Grange, near Faringdon in Berkshire. The proprietor, Mr. Yate, was then in London, a prisoner for his religion, and his mother lived at Lyford in the company of two priests named Ford and Collington, and some Brigittine nuns to whom he was giving protection. Yate had more than once begged Campion to visit them, but the household was notorious, and, since it was already liberally supplied with priests, Campion had hitherto declined. Now, however, that he was to pass so near them, Campion asked permission to stop there the night. Persons distrusted the plan. He knew Campion's gentle courtesy and the tenacity of pious women. They would never let him leave. Campion's heart was set upon the visit; he promised to stay exactly as long as Persons ordered; he offered to put himself under obedience to the lay-brother Ralph Emerson, who was to be his companion to Norfolk. On these terms Persons gave his permission, and the two parted, this time for life.

All went well at Lyford. Campion behaved with complete discretion; he refused to preach or to be displayed in any way to the neighbours; he conferred with the good women, quietly, one by one, said Mass for them early next day, and departed unobtrusively towards Oxford in the company of Father Collington, before anyone outside the house got wind of his arrival.

Lyford, with its nuns and its two chaplains, was the religious centre of the district. That afternoon there were callers. Catholic gossip began, and the women could not contain their news; the famous Father Campion had been there; he had said this and that; he had dressed in such a way; this was how he had heard confessions; it was thus he had said Mass; they might have passed him on the road; he was barely thirty miles away at the moment.

The neighbours were chagrined at what they had missed; how could the women have been so churlish as to keep their guest to themselves? And he had not preached? Everyone said it was the experience of a lifetime to hear him. Father Campion must be brought back.

Ford was mounted and sent after him. They met that evening at an inn near Oxford, where he was already in discussion with a group of undergraduates and masters of the university. He was weary of danger, and took risks in these last days that he would not have allowed himself a year before. The company had already tried to get a sermon out of him. Now Ford arrived with his entreaty to return to Lyford. Campion referred then to 'the little man', his superior. They all turned upon Brother Ralph, arguing and coaxing. Obedience must be tempered with good sense; the object of Persons' order was the good of souls. Here was an unrivalled opportunity. He had allowed Campion to waste a day among a handful of pious women; now he was offered a large and eager audience. Brother Ralph pleaded the necessity of the road. Here he was undone. Persons had expressly forbidden Campion to preach or visit in Lancashire; for him the journey was an unnecessary risk and waste of energy. Let him stay at Lyford over the week-end, while Brother Ralph fetched the papers from Mr. Houghton. Campion could leave on Sunday and meet him at a Catholic gentleman's house on the borders of Norfolk. Brother Ralph yielded and rode on alone into Lancashire. Campion returned, joyfully attended, to the house at Lyford.

The Grange still stands, reduced in size and importance, but still a house of poignant association to the Catholic visitor. At this date it occupied four sides of a courtyard with a gate-tower, long since demolished, facing a drawbridge. Mrs. Yate's room and the priest's cell have disappeared, and there is no good reason for identifying the long room as the chapel. The moat and drawbridge posts can still be seen and a line of trees marks the avenue which once constituted the main approach. Originally the moat enclosed a large area which included a dove-cot, probably other outbuildings, and a dense orchard and fruit garden. The fact, which will be seen later, that it employed sixty men seven or eight hours to search it, attests the size of the place.

Friday and Saturday passed without alarm. Campion was lionized and cosseted by the good ladies; scholars came out from Oxford, and the Catholic neighbours flocked to see him. On Sunday, in obedience to Brother Ralph, he was to start for Norfolk. That morning Mr. George Eliot arrived. He was a typical member of the class of professional priest-hunter whom Cecil and Walsingham now employed. Originally a manservant of low character, he had worked in the households of Mr. Roper of Orpington, in Kent, and the Dowager Lady Petre, mother of Sir John Petre of Ingatestone, Essex, both of whom were Catholic. While in their service he had professed himself of their Faith. He got into trouble for rape and homicide and left Lady Petre's employment for jail. From there, he wrote several letters to Leicester offering information against his former employers, giving a list of prominent Catholics, and in particular accusing Father Payne, who lived in Roper's house under the title of steward, of a 'horrible treason' by which the priest proposed to levy a certain company of armed men, fall upon and dispatch Leicester, Walsingham and Burghley, use Her Majesty in such sort as neither modesty nor duty would suffer him to rehearse and raise a general cry everywhere of 'Queen Mary! Queen Mary!' No anti-Catholic tale was too extravagant or insubstantial to interest the Council; Eliot was summoned to Leicester House, given his freedom and a general commission to seek out and arrest any Jesuits or massing priests whom he could discover. A man named David Jenkins was appointed to assist him. Profiting by his former Catholic connexion, he was able to attend and report a Mass said at Haddon, in Oxfordshire, on 2 July, and, still on the same errand, returned to the neighbourhood at the time of Campion's visit. Lyford was well known as a Catholic centre, and in the hope of finding a Mass there on the Sunday morning he and Jenkins arrived, quite unaware of the sensational coup they were about to make.

On their approach at about eight in the morning, they found the gates barred and a watchman on guard. Thomas Cooper, the cook, had been a fellow-servant with Eliot at Mr. Roper's. Eliot asked for him by name, and the watchman, who at first had received them with suspicion, went in to fetch him. Eliot and Jenkins waited in their saddles outside the gates. Presently the cook came out. They greeted each other as old friends. Eliot explained that he was on his way to Derbyshire, and must now be off.

'No,' said the cook, 'that you shall not do before dinner.'

Eliot and Jenkins made a show of reluctance, but at length allowed themselves to be persuaded; dismounted, and accompanied the cook to the buttery, where he drew them a jug of ale.

Presently after [Eliot records], the said Cook came and whispered with me, and asked, Whether my friend (meaning the said Jenkins) were within the Church or not?

To which I answered, 'He was not; but yet,' said I, 'he is a very honest man, and one that wishes well that way.'

Then said the Cook to me, 'Will you go up?' By which speech I knew he would bring me to a Mass.

And I assured him and said, 'Yea, for God's sake, that let me do; for seeing I must needs tarry, let me take something with me that is good.'

Accordingly they left Jenkins in the buttery with his beer mug, and passing through the hall, the dining parlour and two or three other rooms, came to a 'fair, large chamber' where Mass was in progress. Father Ford—who was known to Eliot by the name of Satwell—was at the altar; the congregation consisted of three nuns, in their habits, thirty-seven lay people, Collington and Campion. Eliot slipped into a place and followed the service with a suitable display of familiarity and devotion. When Ford's Mass was finished, the people remained on their knees while Campion vested, said his Mass,

and at the end thereof, made holy bread and delivered it to the people there, to everyone some, together with holy water; whereof he gave [Eliot] part also.

And then was there a chair set in the chamber something beneath the Altar, wherein the said Campion did sit down; and there made a Sermon very nigh an hour long; the effect of the text being, as I remember, 'That Christ wept over Jerusalem, etc.' And so applied the same to this our country of England for that the Pope his authority and doctrine did not so flourish here as the same Campion desired.

The text was from the gospel of the day; from that morning every phrase of the reproach was indelibly written in the hearts of Campion's audience, 'Jerusalem, Jerusalem, thou that killest the prophets'. It was the Tenebrae of his Passion. Never, it was remembered, had his eloquence been more compelling than in this last sermon.

While he listened Eliot's hand strayed, he tells us, to the pocket where he kept the Queen's commission; it was half in his mind to produce it there and then; but he prudently sat the sermon out, and as soon as he decently could, hurried back to Jenkins in the buttery. There was no time now to stay for dinner, and making what excuses they could to the hospitable cook, the two galloped off with their news to the nearest Justice.

Seven or eight of the visiting Catholics remained for dinner, and they were still at the table, at about one o'clock, when the alarm was given that the house was completely surrounded. Mr. Fettiplace, a neighbouring magistrate, Eliot, Jenkins and a squadron of soldiers sat their horses outside the main gate demanding admission, while the watchmen reported armed men posted in a circle round the moat. Campion wished to surrender himself, in the hope that, content with his easy capture, the magistrate might leave the others unmolested. Mrs. Yate insisted that the house was well provided with hiding-places, and that there was a fair prospect of escape; in any case his presence there would ruin them all, whether he surrendered or was discovered. The three priests were led to a secret room, where there was just space for them to lie side by side on a couch; some provisions were put in with them and the panelling slid into place; meanwhile the nuns hastily put themselves into ordinary costume; books, beads, pictures were hidden away; Edward Yate, brother of the master of the house, and two yokels, locked themselves in the pigeon house; it was half an hour before Fettiplace was admitted. He was then greeted by Mrs. Yate and her guests—five gentlemen, one gentlewoman and the three nuns in lay attire—who demanded indignantly to know the reason for the disturbance. Eliot accused the entire party of having been present at a Mass that morning. They flatly denied it, and Fettiplace found himself in the difficult position of having to choose between the word of a professional informer and of a number of local gentry. Perhaps he knew that Eliot was telling the truth, but he had no particular zeal to prove it. Eliot insisted on a search, and the men marched through the house, glancing under beds and behind curtains. Nothing was found; the magistrate had done his duty and was ready to apologize and withdraw. But, says Eliot, 'I eftsoone put Master Fettiplace in remembrance of our Commission.' The magistrate protested that he had no warrant to do any damage in the house. Eliot produced his commission and began to read an authorization for this very purpose. One of the men, looking over his shoulder, discovered that he was inventing. Eliot challenged the magistrate to arrest him as a comforter of Jesuits. They were now outside the gates, arguing the matter on the drawbridge; within, the household was jubilant at their escape. Suddenly the party were observed to waver and turn back; they were demanding readmission. Eliot had won. Fettiplace recognized that he was a dangerous man; a malicious report to Leicester might bring about his own ruin.

Eliot and Jenkins took charge of the raid. Edward Yate and the two countrymen were discovered in the dove-cot. It was now useless to pretend that nothing unusual had been on foot. Methodically, room by room, they went through the house, sounding the panelling and splintering it where it seemed hollow; they found several secret places, but no trace of the priests. The afternoon drew in, and Fettiplace's men became sulky. Eliot sent to the High Sheriff, Mr. Foster, and to another Justice, Mr. Wiseman, for further help. Foster, who had no liking for this sort of procedure, sent back word that he could not be found; Wiseman arrived before dark with a posse of a dozen of his own servants 'very able men,' according to Eliot, 'and well appointed'. That night a guard of sixty was set about the house, while others slept on the premises; Mrs. Yate gave them supper.

The cell where the priests lay opened out of 'a chamber near the top of the house; which was but very simple; having in it a large shelf with divers tools and instruments both upon it and hanging by it; which they judged to belong to some cross bow maker'. Shelves hung across the door. Mrs. Yate had her bed made up in a room close to this workshop, and during the night Campion came out and addressed a few words of encouragement there to the household. As they were leaving her room one of them stumbled; the guard was alarmed, but the priests got back to their hiding-place without detection.

At daybreak the search began again, but by now even Eliot was losing heart. He knew that Campion had been there, and had meant to remain to dinner, but it seemed probable that he had changed his plan—perhaps alarmed by Eliot's precipitate departure—and had escaped while his pursuers were summoning Fettiplace. When they were 'in effect clear void of any hope', Jenkins noticed a chink of light in the well over the stairs, and seizing a crowbar, revealed the back of the cell,

> The priests lying all close together upon a bed of purpose laid for them; where they had bread, meat and drink sufficient to have relieved them three or four days together.
>
> The said Jenkins then called very loudly, and said 'I have found the traitors!' and presently company enough was with him; who there saw the said Priests, when there was no remedy for them but *nolens volens* courteously yielded themselves.

PART IV
THE MARTYR

THE MARTYR

As soon as the news of the discovery reached him, the High Sheriff, Humphrey Foster, rode over from Aldermaston to take charge of the house. He saw to it that Campion and the other prisoners were decently used, and dispatched a messenger to the Court for further instructions. Eliot, however, had anticipated him, arrived first with the news and was given, as was very clearly his right, full credit for the capture. Before Thursday he was back at Lyford with authority to bring Campion and the men taken with him to London as his own prisoners. The Sheriff was instructed to provide a guard. In Eliot's absence there had been another arrest, of a fourth priest named William Filby, who, unwittingly, came to call at Lyford and found the magistrates in possession.

The party set out on the 20th, passed through Abingdon, and rested the first night at Henley. At every stage of the journey large numbers turned out to see them, some with open sympathy. Persons was still in hiding at Stonor; he sent his servant to see how Campion was looking, and the man brought back word that his gentleness and charm had already put him on easy terms with his captors. The party dined together at the same table. Campion chatted easily with them and with several members of the university who were allowed to approach him.

Eliot was ignored; neither magistrates nor soldiers troubled to hide their dislike of the man; once or twice on the road there had been hostile movements in the crowd as the informer passed, and cries of 'Judas'; his first elation was exhausted; the praise which he had received at Court sounded faint and distorted; it was almost as though this were Campion's triumph, and he the malefactor. At last he could bear Campion's neglect no longer, and so broke out: 'Mr. Campion, you look cheerfully upon everyone but me. I know you are angry with me for this work.'

Then, perhaps for the first time since Sunday morning, when Eliot had knelt after Mass to receive the holy bread from his hands, Campion turned his eyes on him, 'God forgive thee, Eliot,' he said, 'for so judging of me; I forgive thee and in token thereof, I drink to thee.' He raised his cup, and then added more gravely, 'Yea, and if thou repent and come to confession, I will absolve thee; but large penance must thou have.'

According to Eliot, Campion warned him that no good would result from the service he had done; which prediction Eliot, as was his nature, took as a threat of Catholic vengeance; from that day he imagined he was being followed and bewitched, and, though no attempt was ever made at reprisal, went in fear of his life, so that the report gained credence that he had lost his wits.

At Henley, that night, after they had all retired to bed, there was a sudden wild shouting; the guards took alarm that an attempt was being made to rescue the prisoners; torches were brought and it was found that Father Filby was suffering from nightmare; he had dreamed that someone was ripping down his body and taking out his bowels.

They spent the succeeding night at Colebrook and there, on special instructions from the Council, the character of the procession was altered. The prisoners were pinioned on their horses; their elbows being tied behind them and their wrists in front; their ankles were strapped together under the horses' bellies. Campion was driven on in front with a paper stuck in his hat reading *CAMPION THE SEDITIOUS JESUIT*. In this way they were paraded through the London streets, crowded for the Saturday market. At Cheapside, the statues at the foot of the old cross were all defaced by the Protestants, but the cross itself still stood beyond their reach. As he passed it, Campion made a low reverence. Finally they reached the Tower, where the Governor, Sir Owen Hopton, took them into his custody. Before he parted with the Berkshire guard, who had had no responsibility for his humiliation, Campion thanked them and blessed them. Then the gates of the Tower shut behind him.

The conditions of imprisonment in the Tower were very different from the sociable, haphazard life at the Marshalsea. The regulations for solitary confinement are on record; the windows were blocked up; light and ventilation came through a 'slope tunnel', barred at top and bottom, so that nothing could be conveyed to the prisoner from outside. The lieutenant had to be present whenever a keeper entered the cell, and it was rarely possible, and then only under the strictest supervision, for prisoners to receive a visitor. In some cases, no doubt, severity was tempered by venality, but Campion was a prisoner of the highest importance, suspect of having wide, subterranean connexions, and Hopton treated him with more than customary harshness. He was placed in the Little Ease, the cell, still an object of interest in the Tower dungeons, in which it was impossible for a full-grown man to stand erect or lie at full length. Here, crouching in the half-dark, he remained for four days. Then the cage was opened and he was summoned to emerge; under a strong guard he was led up to the level of the ground, out into the air and sunshine, across the yard to the water gate, where a boat awaited them; they rowed up-stream among the ferrymen and barges and busy river traffic. Presently they reached Leicester House.

We cannot know what hopes may have stirred in Campion's heart as he recognized the home of his old friend and patron; as the guard led him through the familiar, frequented anterooms to the Earl's apartment. The doors were thrown open; the soldiers at his side stiffened; they were in the presence of the Queen. Beside her chair stood Leicester, Bedford and two Secretaries of State. The guards stood back and Campion advanced to make his salutations.

It was a singular meeting.

The grime of the dungeon was still on Campion; his limbs as he knelt were stiff from his imprisonment.

The vast red wig nodded acknowledgement; the jewels and braid and gold lace glittered and the sunken, painted face smiled in recognition. They received him courteously, almost affectionately.

There is none that knoweth me familiarly [Campion had written to Leicester ten years earlier] but he knoweth withal how many ways I have been beholden to your lordship. How often at Oxford, how often at the Court, how at Rycote, how at Windsor, how by letters, how by reports, you have not ceased to further with advice and to countenance with authority, the hope and expectation of me, a single student.

Campion had followed other advice, recognized another authority, in those ten years; he had lived in a different hope and expectation; he stood before them now as an outcast, momentarily interrupted in his passage from the dungeon to the scaffold. But, for the occasion, politeness was maintained.

They questioned him about his purpose in coming to England, about Persons, about his instructions from Rome. He answered easily and quietly; he had come for the salvation of souls. The harsh, peremptory tones of Elizabeth broke in; did he acknowledge her as his Queen or not? Campion replied that he did indeed recognize her as his lawful Queen and governess, and was bound to her in obedience in all temporal matters. She pressed him with the question of her deposition. He answered, with perfect candour, that it was a subject upon which theologians were still divided, and began to explain the distinction between the *potestas ordinata* and *potestas inordinata* of the Papacy, and quoted the text, 'Render unto Caesar the things that are Caesar's'.

But the politicians were not in the mood for a debate upon Canon Law. They were satisfied that he had no treasonable designs, and told him that they had no fault to find with him except that he was a Papist.

'Which is my greatest glory,' Campion replied.

They then made the proposal for which he had been summoned. The past ten years should be forgotten; the road of preferment was still open; if he would publicly adjure his Faith and enter the Protestant ministry there was still no limit to the heights he might reach. The offer was kind in its intention. They had no desire to kill the virtuous and gifted man who had once been their friend, a man, moreover, who could still be of good service to them. From earliest youth, among those nearest them, they had been used to the spectacle of men who would risk their lives for power, but to die deliberately, without hope of release, for an idea, was something beyond their comprehension. They knew that it happened; they had seen it in the preceding reign, but not among people of their own acquaintance; humble, eccentric men had gone to the stake; argumentative men had gone into exile in Germany and Geneva, but Elizabeth and Cecil and Dudley had quietly conformed to the prevailing fashion; they had told their beads and eaten fish on Fridays, confessed and taken communion. Faith—as something concrete and indestructible, of such transcendent value that, once it was held, all other possessions became a mere encumbrance—was unknown to them; in rare, pensive moments shadows loomed and flickered across their minds, sentiment, conscience, fear of the unknown; some years Leicester patronized the Catholics, at others 'the Family of Love'; Elizabeth looked now on the crucifix, now on a talisman; Bible and Demonology lay together beside her bed. What correspondence, even in their charity, could they have with Campion?

He returned to the Tower, and, five days later, Leicester and Burghley signed the warrant to put him to the torture.

From now until 1 December, when he was dragged out to Tyburn, Campion disappeared from the world. He was seen again at the Conference in September with the Anglican clergy, and at his trial in November, but of the agony and endurance of those four months we have only hints and fragments of information. The little that we know was hidden from his contemporaries, and rumour was busy with his name.

First it was said that he had turned Protestant, had accepted a bishopric, and was about to make a public avowal of his apostasy and burn the *Ten Reasons* at St. Paul's Cross. Hopton himself seems to have been responsible for this report, and so authoritatively that it was made an official announcement at many of the pulpits of London. Then it was said that he had taken his own life; then that he had purchased his safety by accusing his former friends of treason. No one was allowed to see him. All over the country gentlemen were being arrested and charged with Catholicism on Campion's authority. His friends were thrown into despair and shame. The Protestants taunted them with their champion's treachery. Then he reappeared, at the Conferences, at his trial, at Tyburn. In those brief glimpses they recognized the man whom they had known and trusted, the old gentleness, the old inflexible constancy. Opinion veered again; the confessions were challenged and could not be produced. They were denounced as forgeries. Only in recent years, when the archives are open and the bitter passions still, can we begin to pierce the subterranean gloom and guess at the atrocious secrets of the torture chamber.

Two things seem certain, that Campion told something and that he told very little. The purpose of his captors was to make him convict himself and his friends of treason, and in this they failed absolutely. Hardened criminals, at the mere sight of the rack, would break down and testify to whatever their jailers demanded. Campion, the gentle scholar, was tortured on three occasions and said nothing that was untrue; nothing to which he was bound in secrecy by the seal of confession; nothing which, in the actual event, brought disaster to anyone. He seems, however, to have made certain admissions with which his scrupulous conscience, always more ready with accusation than with excuse, troubled him on the scaffold.

These all dealt with the hospitality he had received during his mission. His first examination took place on 30 or 31 July, and immediately afterwards Burghley wrote to Lord Shrewsbury that 'he would confess nothing of moment'. The subject upon which the Council particularly desired a 'confession' was the sum of £30,000 which he was reputed to have conveyed to the rebels in Ireland, how the money had been collected, how transferred. On this topic they could obtain no information. Immediately afterwards, however, they had knowledge of names of several people associated with Campion. On 2 August Burghley drew up a list of his hosts in Lancashire, on the 4th in Yorkshire, the 6th in Northamptonshire, and 7th and 14th in Derbyshire. He attributed these to Campion's confessions. Thirty-two persons in all were questioned as a result of the lists, but in no case was the evidence considered strong enough for a conviction.

What importance Campion's admissions had in the compilation, and how those admissions were extorted, cannot be certainly known, but it is possible to make a conjecture.

The examiners were men proficient in every trick of their profession, and they were already well informed from other sources. For months the pursuit had been closing in; there had been other arrests; the two servants, taken at Lyford, had turned Queen's evidence. For over a year spies had been at work all over the country bribing and threatening; indiscreet conversations at the Marshalsea had been overheard; scraps of information from countless sources had been collected and arranged. Before the examination began the Crown lawyers had a fair idea of Campion's movements.

All the devices of cross-examination were then employed. They would pretend to certain knowledge, where they had only a suspicion—'When you were at such-and-such a house you spoke about Mary Queen of Scots'; 'No, we spoke only of religion'; 'Then you *were* at that house'—they would quote to him spurious confessions of others; they would tell him of arrests that had not been made, of false betrayals. All the bluffs and traps which, in a court of law, will confuse a witness, cool-headed and protected by counsel, were now used upon a man stretched in the last extremity of physical agony.

It is certain that neither then, nor in his subsequent examinations, did Campion ever break down. He never blurted out all that he knew, anything his tormentors required of him, only so that he might be released from the unendurable pain. There are no signed depositions. It was the custom of the time for the clerk, seated beside the rack, to record all that the witness said; then, when he was released, as soon as his fingers could hold a pen, he was required to put his name at the foot of each sheet. The pitiful, straggling, barely recognizable signatures were then admissible as evidence. In Campion's case they could produce no such testimony; if in the last minutes before the senses failed, in the delirium of pain before unconsciousness gratefully intervened and he was taken inert from the rack; as the pitiless questioning went on and on and the body lost its dependence upon the will—if then he spoke of things that should have been kept secret, his first conscious act was to repudiate them; the confessions were useful as a bluff to use against other prisoners, but they were valueless in a court of law.

And, even so, it was very little that was wrung from him. A page survives in Burghley's handwriting summarizing the investigation.

> Henry Perpoynt esquire.
> Jervis Perpoint his brother.
> Campyon. That he was there all the last Christmas and tarried there until the tewsday after twelfth day, brought thither by Jervis Pierpoynt.
> Confessed by bothe the Pierpoynts he said masses and confessed Jervis every week once.
> Henry Sacheverell esquire.
> Campyon. That he was there aboute the wednesday after twelfth day last, tarried there one night.

Confessed by Mr. Sacheverell and that he said one masse.

The Lady ffuljames.

Campyon. That he was there one night about Saturdaie after twelfth day last.

Jervis Perpoynt that they stayed there two nights and said two masses.

And so on. These are not the confessions of a man whose courage has failed; it was not the kind of information that the rack-master was trying to wring from him; the Council wanted tales of Spanish gold and poisoned bodkins if the execution were to be popular.

It was recognized that the itinerary was incomplete and the details inadequate. On 7 August the Council dispatched to the Earl of Huntingdon a list of some of Campion's Yorkshire hosts with instructions to examine

> bothe of them and others of their familyes and neighbourhood . . . how long he continued in their said houses or anie others, from where he came, whither he went and with whom; how often he or anie other jesuite or priest said anie masse in their houses . . . whether they themselves or anie other have heard masse or been reconciled or confessed.

On the back of the letter was a list similar to the one quoted:

> Campion confesseth he was in the City of York at the house of D. Vavasour. Thither resorted soche of the neighbours as Mrs. Vavasour called her husband being

then in prison. He was also at the house of one Mrs.
Boulmer. He hath forgotten who brought him thither
neither did he know the company, etc.

The Vavasours were notorious recusants; their house
would be under surveillance; Dr. Vavasour was in prison
for his religion; it was a common practice to shut up a spy
with the prisoners to gain their confidence; a secret note
from his wife may have fallen into the jailer's hands. There
are many ways in which the Council might have information about Campion's visit. But of the details which only
Campion could tell, the waverers who conformed in public
to the State Church but came to him secretly for advice,
there is not a word. 'He hath forgotten who brought him
thither.' One can guess what efforts were made to stimu-
late his memory; what endurance and triumph is recorded in
that phrase.

It will be seen from the above quotations that Campion
very rarely admitted to having performed any priestly
office, and without that admission the case against his hosts
was extremely slender. The recent proclamation had made
it treasonable to harbour a priest, but Campion had travelled
in disguise and under an assumed name. In the open hospitality of the age, the mere fact of Campion having slept under
a certain roof was not enough to convict the master of com-
plicity. Persons' letter, quoted in the preceding chapter,
shows that he frequently stayed, unsuspected, in the houses
of irreproachable Protestants.

But the men who were now arrested and questioned on
the authority of Campion's 'confessions' had no means of

judging the weakness of the case against them. They were
told that Campion had betrayed them. The news reached
Pounde in prison, and, impetuous as ever, he wrote a letter
to Campion, which his jailer accepted a bribe to deliver.
The whole incident is obscure. He may have written in
reproach or in inquiry about the authenticity of the 'confessions'. In any case, the message was shown to Hopton
who, having read it, told the man to deliver it to Campion
and bring him back the answer. This note has not been
preserved, nor have we any exact transcript of its terms; it
was quoted at the trial of Lord Vaux, Tresham, Catesby and
others before the Star Chamber as follows:

> A letter produced, said to be intercepted, which Mr.
> Campion should seem to write to a fellow prisoner of
> his, namely, Mr. Pound; wherein he did take notice
> that by frailty he had confessed of some houses where
> he had been, which now he repented him, and desired
> Mr. Pound to beg pardon of the Catholics therein,
> saying that in this he rejoiced, that he had discovered
> no things of secret, nor would he, come rack, come
> rope.

Without Pounde's letter, to which it was a reply, this message is capable of more than one interpretation. Its value to
the Council was as evidence of conspiracy, 'the things of
secret' being taken as a political plot. The plainest and most
probable meaning would seem to be that by 'frailty', either
of endurance or astuteness, Campion had been forced into
admissions which he now repented, but that he had merely
confirmed what they already knew and had given no new

information to the inquisitors—nothing that had hitherto been secret to them. His anxiety was not to defend his own reputation, but to warn his friends against an attempt to bluff them, as he had himself been bluffed.

One other point must be noticed with regard to the 'confessions'. At the beginning of his Conferences with the Anglican clergy there was some discussion of Campion's treatment on the rack. Beale, the Clerk of the Council, asked if he had been examined on any point of religion. Campion answered, 'that he was not indeed directly examined of religion, but moved to confess in what places he had been conversant since his repair into the realm'. Beale replied, 'that this was required of him because many of his fellows and by likelihood himself also, had reconciled divers of her Highnesses subjects to the Romish Church'. To which Campion replied:

> That forasmuch as the Christians of old time being commanded to deliver up the books of their religion to such as persecuted them, refused so to do, and misliked with them that did so, calling them *traditores,* he might not betray his Catholic brethren which were, as he said, the temples of the Holy Ghost.

Now Beale himself had been present at the racking; Hopton, Hammond and Norton, the other examiners, were present in the Conference room. The chief purpose of the meeting was to discredit Campion publicly in every way they could. And yet when he made this provocative comparison of himself with the Christian martyrs in ancient Rome, no one retorted that he *had* betrayed his brethren, the temples of the Holy Ghost, and out of his own mouth was condemned as *traditor*. Instead the question was immediately dropped. The examiners did not wish to give Campion the opportunity of challenging the 'confessions' that were being circulated under his name.

The Conferences referred to above were four in number. They were held at the express orders of the Council, who were anxious that Campion's challenge, contained in the *Brag* and the *Ten Reasons,* should not seem to go unanswered. Aylmer, Bishop of London, chose the disputants.

The first took place in the Tower of London on 1 September. No opportunity was given to Campion to prepare himself; he was roused without warning, unfettered and led from his cell. Sherwin, Bosgrave, Pounde and some other Catholic prisoners were waiting under escort. They may well have supposed that their hour had come, and that they were being taken to summary execution. Instead they were marched to the chapel, where they found a formidable array drawn up to meet them. On one side a State box had been erected in which lounged members of the Court and Council; opposite stood a table littered with books and papers, behind which were enthroned two clergymen, in starched linen and voluminous, academic robes. They were Nowell, the Dean of St. Paul's, and Day, the Dean of Windsor; round them sat a number of chaplains and clerks, helping to arrange the notes and mark the passages to be quoted. Another table, and other high chairs, accommodated Charke and Dr. Whitaker, the Regius Professor of Divinity at Cambridge, who were to act as notaries. The Governor of the Tower sat with the rack-master and other officials; a large and varied audience filled every available space, for theological dispute was a popular recreation of the day. Some Catholics were in the crowd, one of whom took notes which furnished Bombinus with the material for his description. The official reports, both of this and the subsequent Conferences, were not published until two years after Campion's death. The Anglicans had then the opportunity to revise them, and one editor, Field, admitted in his preface, 'If Campion's answers be thought shorter than they were, you must know that he had much waste speech, which, being impertinent, is now omitted.' Throughout all the Conferences Campion shows constant anxiety that he is not being reported justly.

A little stool was set for him among the soldiers in the body of the court. He had now been in solitary confinement for five weeks; his second examination under torture had taken place ten days before and, though he was gradually recovering the use of his limbs, his health was broken. The Catholic witness reports that his face was colourless, 'his memory destroyed and his force of mind almost extinguished'. With unconscious irony the Dean of St. Paul's opened the discussion by blandly rebuking Campion for having, in his *Ten Reasons,* dared to accuse the Queen's most merciful Government of *'inusitata supplicia'*—'uncommon cruelty'—and the Anglican bishops of offering *'tormenta non scholas'*—'tortures instead of conference'.

Campion replied by protesting against the manifest inequality of the contest, his own lack of preparation, his deprivation of texts and notes. It was here that the subject of his 'confessions' was raised, and hastily shelved, as described above.

The Deans then proceeded to the debate, the scheme of which was that they should propose the subjects, taken from the *Ten Reasons*, should state their argument in the form of a syllogism, and Campion should answer them. In this way, with a recess for dinner, they continued until nightfall. The chief topic was the Anglican defence of Luther's doctrine of Justification by Faith alone. The report makes tedious and shameful reading, and the results were inconclusive. Campion was freely insulted, described as *os impudens* and *miles gloriosus*, and any demonstration in his favour was instantly checked by the soldiers. Only twice did he seem clearly to be in the wrong. He was unable to verify his quotation from Luther, describing the Epistle of St. James as 'a thing of straw'. It occurred in the Jena edition, from which he had taken it, but not in the expurgated Wittenberg edition, with which he was now provided. The second occasion was when he became confused in a passage from the Greek Testament, and refused to continue the argument. His opponents eagerly seized upon this, and both now and later asserted that his much-advertised scholarship was spurious. Apologists have suggested that the type was too small for him to read, but the simplest explanation is that his Greek was, in fact, rather rusty. He was pre-eminently a Latinist. He had read Greek at Oxford and Douai, could quote it familiarly and write it in a clear and scholarly hand—of this there is abundant proof —but he had used it little at Prague, and, when he did so, spoke it with the Bohemian accent which was confusing in England. He regarded the Conference as a test of the truth of his creed, not of his own accomplishments, and he was unwilling to compromise his case by straying on uncertain ground. At the end of the day, when the Catholics returned to the cells and the Deans to their comfortable lodgings, both sides were satisfied that they had had the best of it.

Eighteen days passed, but Campion, in his sunless dungeon, had lost count of time, and, lying in constant prayer, thought that it had been only a week, when he was again led out to debate. This time his opponents were Dr. Goode, the Provost of King's College, Cambridge, and William Fulke, the popular preacher whose delight at the execution of Dr. Storey has been reported earlier in this narrative. Fulke was a contemporary of Campion's, and had been his unsuccessful rival for the silver pen offered to the prize boy at the City schools. He was an enthusiastic opponent of the surplice, and had inflamed a riot at the university on that subject which led to his being sent down; he was triumphantly reinstated in 1567, but was again expelled for conniving at an incestuous marriage; Court favour did not fail him, and in 1569 he was restored to his fellowship, became Leicester's chaplain, a Doctor of Divinity by Royal Mandate, and Master of Pembroke Hall, where he augmented the Master's stipend by cutting down the number of fellowships. From 1580 he was in regular employment as an official Anglican controversialist, both against Catholics and the more extreme Protestants of the 'Family of Love'.

On this occasion the Conference took place in greater privacy, in Hopton's Hall, but the method was the same as before, the Anglicans stating their arguments and Campion objecting. In the morning the Anglicans set themselves to deny the existence of a visible Church; in the afternoon to prove that the Church was capable of error. As before, Campion was forbidden to take any lead, and when he attempted to press an argument was sharply reprimanded. 'It is your part to answer, not to oppose', and Campion replied wearily, 'I have answered, but I wish to God I had a notary. Well, I commit it all to God.'

In the afternoon the dispute veered again to Justification by Works. Campion asserted that children who died without sin, were saved. The Anglicans maintained the contrary doctrine that they were damned unless specially 'elected'; that baptism had no power to save.

Only at rare moments did the dialogue become animated:

GOODE: Can you love God above all things and your neighbour as yourself? Can you love him with all your heart, with all your soul and with all your strength?

CAMPION: I can. For when I prefer God before all things and love him chiefly, I love him above all.

FULKE: Note that blasphemous absurdity.

GOODE: If a man may fulfil the law to justification, then Christ died in vain. . . .

CAMPION: Why think you the law was given to no purpose? I am sure it was given to be fulfilled, and we are not bidden to keep it, if it were impossible.

FULKE: The law was given for another case . . . namely to show us our infirmity, that we may be convicted of sin.

CAMPION: You will give me leave to declare my meaning.

FULKE: Belike you have an ill opinion of the audience that they can understand nothing except you tell them twenty times over. If you will not suffer me to proceed, I must desire Master Lieutenant to command you.

Campion was never allowed to forget the difference of position between himself and his opponents.

Later in the afternoon the Anglicans were denying the Real Presence in the Mass, saying that the doctrine denied the bodily resurrection of Christ. Campion broke out impatiently, 'What? Will you make Him a prisoner now in Heaven? Must He be bound to those properties of a natural body? Heaven is His palace and you will make it His prison.'

GOODE: They are the words of the Holy Ghost. It becometh not you to jest at them and specially considering your state being a prisoner.

It is clear, however, even in the official report, that Campion acquitted himself the better. Once he was tripped up in his Greek, giving the wrong name to the tense of κεκλειομενον, but the general debate had been of the broad and humane truths of the ancient faith, rather than of small details of text and verse, and the disadvantage of his circumstances oppressed him less.

The debate was continued five days later. Both sides were now out of patience with one another. 'You are very imperious,' Campion complained. 'You come, I trow, to prove me as a grammar scholar and to take me up with check at your pleasure. I know no cause why I should take it at your hands. I am the Queen's prisoner, not yours.'

As before, the form of the syllogism was used:

> FULKE: Whatever is in the sacrament is void of sense or insensible: But Christ is not insensible: *Ergo* Christ is not in the sacrament.

But there was now little pretence of serious academic dispute. The farce had to be played out; that was the Council's order; but neither side hoped for any profit at the outcome.

Campion was consistently refused the courtesies of debate. 'If you dare, let me show you Augustine and Chrysostom,' he cried at one moment, 'if you dare.'

> FULKE: Whatever you can bring, I have answered already in writing against others of your side. And yet if you think you can add anything, put it in writing and I will answer it.
>
> CAMPION: Provide me with ink and paper and I will write.
>
> FULKE: I am not to provide you ink and paper.
>
> CAMPION: I mean, procure me that I may have liberty to write.
>
> FULKE: I know not for what cause you are restrained of that liberty, and therefore I will not take upon me to procure it.
>
> CAMPION: Sue to the Queen that I may have liberty to oppose. I have been now thrice opposed. It is reason that I should oppose once.
>
> FULKE: I will not become a suitor for you.

So the futile debate continued until dusk; Campion was led back to his cell; the divines collected their notes and sauntered home to supper, to boast to their womenfolk how they had rattled the Jesuit; but under their windows the chapmen and balladmongers were already hawking a different version:

A Jesuit, a Jebusite? Wherefore I you pray?
Because he doth teach you the only right way?
He professeth the same by learning to prove
And shall we from learning to rack him remove.

His reasons were ready, his grounds were most sure,
The enemy cannot his force long endure,
Campion, in camping on spiritual field,
In God's cause his life is ready to yield.

Our preachers have preached in pastime and pleasure,
And now they be hated for passing all measure;
Their wives and their wealth have made them so mute,
They cannot nor dare not with Campion dispute.

Still the Council was not satisfied, and a fourth Conference was arranged. Two new Anglican champions, Dr. John Walker and Mr. Charke, were put forward. Walker began the day with a denunciation of Campion as 'an unnatural man to his country, degenerate from an Englishman, an apostate in religion, a fugitive from this realm, unloyal to his Prince', who had returned 'to plant secretly the blasphemous Mass'. The old questions of Justification by Faith and Sufficiency of Scripture were proposed. There was little public interest now in the controversy, and when the meagre audience, shamed and bored, attempted to leave, Charke had the doors shut on them so that they should hear him out. He proved Campion wrong in a reference to Tertullian; that was the full extent of his triumph. It was the most ignominious display yet made by the Government party, and after that evening Burghley gave instructions that the Conferences should be discontinued. Campion was left in peace, to prepare himself for death.

A majority in the Council had decided in favour of Campion's execution; under the recent laws his office as priest made him guilty of high treason, but respect for public opinion, both in the country and abroad, made them hesitate to bring him to the scaffold upon this charge alone. Walsingham was in Paris that summer, on an embassy connected with the Queen's marriage; he employed his leisure in interviewing various informers and renegade *émigrés,* and on 20 August he was able to report to Cecil a Popish plot for the conquest of Scotland which was being offered for sale at twenty crowns, but the Council do not seem to have found it suitable. Campion's fate was now curiously linked with that of Anjou, the Queen's 'little frog'. During that summer and autumn the exigencies of foreign policy brought the French marriage into increasing prominence. It was a matter of the greatest delicacy. Catherine of Medici, the Queen Mother, was pressing her son to give up all idea of Elizabeth and to marry a Spanish princess; there was a danger that Elizabeth, who throughout the reign had made it her policy to keep the precarious balance between Spain and France, might find herself isolated against an alliance of the two traditional enemies. Her throne was threatened from both sides, for, at home, it rested upon her personal popularity with her people, and it was doubtful how long her glamour could survive so grotesque a romance. Resentment at the proposal had become vocal, two years earlier, among subjects as different in character as Sir Philip Sidney and Stubbs, the printer. Stubbs's mutilation was remembered by the low-church party. It was rumoured that the Queen was again falling into the hands of the Papists. An emphatic assertion of her Protestant principles was demanded; the death of her Catholic prisoners would conciliate just those elements of the population whom Stubbs's punishment had antagonized. But this would embarrass her negotiations with Anjou; somewhere in his twisted mind the little monster concealed, like the jewel in a toad's head, a genuine loyalty to his Faith. It would be ungracious to greet him on his arrival in England—he was coming on 1 November—with the execution, on purely religious grounds, of a fellow-Catholic of international repute. It was essential to convict Campion of some specific treasonable intent. Accordingly, on 31 October, while Anjou was in the Channel, Campion was again put to the rack in the hope that, at the last moment, he might extricate the Council from their difficulty by confessing to one or other of the plots they had devised for him. So savage were the torturers on this occasion, Campion informed a friend with whom later he had a few words of conversation, that he thought they intended to kill him. He never recovered from this racking; when his keeper asked him next day how he felt, he answered 'Not ill, because not at all', and three weeks later he was unable to lift his hand high enough to take an oath. But Lord Hunsdon reported that one might sooner pluck his heart out of his bosom, than rack a word out of his mouth that he made conscience of uttering. The Council therefore decided to proceed with the trial without further scruple.

The first indictment proposed was that Campion:

> Did traitorously pretend to have power to absolve the subjects of the said Queen from their natural obedience to her majesty, with the intention to withdraw the said subjects of the said Queen from the religion now by her supreme authority established within this realm of England to the Roman religion, and to move the same subjects of the said Queen to promise obedience to the pretensed authority of the Roman See to be used within the dominions of the said Queen

and proceeded to particularize an individual so absolved. The space for this man's name was left blank until a suitable informer could be found to give evidence.

But the considerations suggested above moved the Council to change their ground, and a fresh indictment was drawn up, upon which Campion was finally brought to trial. In this it was asserted that William Allen, Nicholas Morton, Persons and Campion had, at Rome on 31 March of the preceding year, at Rheims on 30 April and on other unspecified days before and after, both at Rome and Rheims, formed a conspiracy to murder Queen Elizabeth; that at Rome, on 20 May and on other dates, they had exhorted foreigners to invade the country; that they had decided to send Persons and Campion into England to stir up a rebellion in support of the invading force.

A further emendation was made, by whose hand it is impossible to tell, and in the margin were inserted the names of Bosgrave, Filby, Ford, Cottam, Lawrence, Richardson, Collington, Sherwin, Kirby, Johnson, Rishton, Briant, Short—the entire bag of priests then in custody—and Orton, a layman, to be tried on the same charge. This addition removes any possibility of believing in the sincerity of the prosecution. It is conceivable that some of the Council believed in the guilt of Allen, Morton, Persons and Campion. That Ford and Collington, who had been in England for the last four or five years, whose only connexion with Campion was that they had been serving a handful of nuns at the house where he was arrested, and Filby, who had dropped in to call, had been dodging about Europe in his company—at Rome on 31 March, at Rheims on 30 April, back at Rome again on 20 May—was a charge which the most cursory investigation must instantly disprove. It was on this indictment, however, that the trial took place.

On Tuesday, 14 November, Campion, Sherwin, Kirby, Bosgrave, Cottam, Johnson, Orton and Rishton were arraigned at the bar of Westminster Hall, and the preposterous charge was first read to them.

'I protest before God and his holy angels,' Campion replied, 'before heaven and earth, before the world and this bar whereat I stand, which is but a small resemblance of the terrible judgement of the next life, that I am not guilty of any part of the treason contained in the indictment, or of any other treason whatever.'

The jury was impanelled for the following Monday. 'Is it possible,' Campion said, 'to find twelve men so wicked and void of all conscience in this city or land that will find us guilty together of this one crime, divers of us never meeting or knowing one the other before our bringing to this bar?'

'The plain reason of our standing here is religion and not treason,' said Sherwin.

Sir Christopher Wray, Chief Justice of the King's Bench: 'The time is not yet come wherein you shall be tried, and therefore you must now spare speech . . . wherefore now plead to the indictment whether you be guilty or not.'

When they were called to take the oath, Campion, as was mentioned above, could not lift his arm; his crippled hands were tucked into the cuffs of his gown, whereupon one of his companions drew up the sleeve, kissed his hand and raised it for him.

Next day Collington, Richardson, Hart, Ford, Filby, Briant and Short were arraigned in the same manner on the same charge.

The trial took place on 20 November. Three gentlemen, originally impanelled as jurymen, refused their attendance, because they doubted that justice would have a free course that day; their places were filled with less scrupulous substitutes. Only one of the twelve dishonoured names has come down to us, one William Lee, the foreman, who was himself an informer and a fanatical Calvinist. Chief Justice Wray presided with gravity and temperance; William Ayloff and, probably, Thomas Gawdy sat with him.

Prisoners at this time were never defended by counsel. The prosecution was in the hands of Mr. Anderson, Queen's Counsel, John Popham, the Attorney-General, cadet of a family already rich in monastic lands, who was later rewarded for his services to the Government by his elevation to the post of Chief Justice of the Queen's Bench, and Thomas Egerton, Solicitor-General, founder of the Ellesmere fortunes.

When the indictment was read, Campion, who acted as spokesman for the prisoners, requested that they might each be given a separate trial. The plea was disallowed.

'I could have wished,' Wray admitted, 'that everyone should have had his special day assigned him, had the time so permitted; but since it cannot be otherwise, we must take it as it is.'

The trial then proceeded in accordance with the Council's instructions.

Anderson opened the case with a general denunciation of the Pope as the Queen's chief enemy, and 'professed scourge of the Gospel'; the prisoners, he said, had lived on the Pope's bounty abroad and were now sent to England as his agents.

Campion indignantly asked whether Mr. Anderson was there as an orator, or as a counsel submitting evidence to a court of law.

THE LORD CHIEF JUSTICE: 'You must have patience with him . . . for they, being of the Queen's Council, speak of no other intent than of duty to Her Majesty.'

Campion again protested that evidence should be brought.

The wisdom and providence of the laws of England, as I take it, is such as proceedeth not to the trial of any man for life and death by shifts of probabilities and conjectural surmises, without proof of the crime by sufficient evidence and substantial witness. I see not to what end Mr. Serjeant's oration tended or if I see an end I see it but frustrate; for be the crime but in trifles, the law hath his passage; be the theft but a halfpenny, witnesses are produced. He barely affirmeth; we flatly deny. . . . Who seeth not but these be odious circumstances to bring a man in hatred with the jury and no necessary matter to conclude him guilty? . . . This word soundeth not a lawyer's usage. . . . These matters ought to be proved and not urged, declared by evidence and not surmised by fancy. Wherefore, in God's behalf, we pray that better proof may be used, and that our lives be not brought in prejudice by conjectures.

Anderson next asserted two oaths taken at the seminaries, one to the Pope, the other to the propositions in a book called Bristow's *Motives*. The confusion resulting from the joint trial was then apparent; it had not yet been proved that any of the prisoners had been to a seminary; in point of fact some had been and some had not; Campion pointed out that in any case the oath was not administered to any except striplings; Bristow's pamphlet was used as a text book only in the elementary course for those who came to the seminary without previous academic training, so that it was entirely beyond the point to argue whether or not it could be held to contain treasonable matter. Kirby protested that of his conscience there were not four copies of Bristow's *Motives* in all the seminaries. There was a general murmur among the prisoners that it was for their religion that they were being tried, not for treason, which Campion voiced, saying that, since they had been offered their liberty on condition of their attending the Anglican services, their faith was the sole cause of their being there.

The question of Bristow's book and the seminary oath was not pressed. Anderson proceeded: 'All of you jointly and severally have received money from the Pope to spend in your journeys. Was such liberality of the Pope's without cause? No, it had an end; and what end should that be but your privy inveighings and persuasions to set on foot his devices and treacheries?'

Campion replied that the end was solely to preach the Gospel.

The first Crown witness was then produced, a man named H. Caddy, of whom little can be traced. He asserted that when he was abroad he was told of a holy vow made between the Pope and two hundred English priests for the restoration of Catholicism. Also that Sir Ralph Shelley, Knight of Malta, had been approached by the Vatican to lead an invading fleet against England and had refused, saying he would sooner drink poison.

Campion easily disposed of this point:

Two hundred priests made an holy vow to labour for the restoring of religion. It seemeth, by all likelihood, that we made up the number, and therefore privy and parties to the treason; here is a conclusion without a jot of affinity to the premises; first an holy vow, then an establishing of religion. What colour is there left here for treason? All the treason rehearsed was reputed to Sir Ralph Shelley; not one syllable thereof was rehearsed to the priests. But granting, and which the witness has not deposed, and namely, that we are some of the two hundred priests; you see Sir Ralph Shelley, a Catholic, the Pope's captain, a layman, would rather drink poison than agree to such treason; it is like that priests . . . would in any wise consent to it. This deposition is more for us than against us.

It was by now abundantly clear that there was to be no fair trial; that the Lords of the Council were demanding a death sentence and that the conviction had to be for treason. But Campion kept up the defence; the trial was being watched all over England. If the Government could announce that the priests had been proved guilty of conspiracy, the Catholic cause would be prejudiced; worse still, the elements among the Catholic laity whose loyalty was already strained by the persecution, would be encouraged in the extreme measures which eventually in the next generation brought about their ruin. The Gunpowder Plot was still at a distance.

Doubtless the priests had heavy secrets to guard; what the rack-master could not discover, we shall never learn. The priests knew, far better than their accusers, the conflict that was rending every Catholic heart in the country. They knew what had been said at those night-long sessions before the morning Mass; what plots they had forbidden in Christ's name; what reasons they had urged to men rendered reckless by injustice; how in private converse and in the inviolable secrecy of the confessional they had wrestled with desperate consciences, holding up the cross, ceaselessly commanding patience, trust, submission, the way of truth that could never be the way of blood. It was these with whom Campion was pleading in the tedious, futile, assertion and denial, perjury and disproof, of the mock trial. He and his fellows were to die, but the world must know the cause.

They accused him of having made himself privy to the Bull of Excommunication, by discussing it with the Cardinal of St. Cecilia; they accused him of association with the Bishop of Ross, whom he had never met; they accused him of private conversation with Dr. Allen, who had been in communication with Dr. Sanders, who was with the Irish rebels.

Campion replied:

> I cannot deny but that I dined with Dr. Allen at Rheims, with whom also after dinner I walked in his garden, spending a time in speeches referred to our old familiarity and acquaintance; during the whole course thereof (I take God to witness) not one jot of our talk glanced to the Crown or State of England; neither had I the least notice of any letters sent to Dr. Sanders.

He was accused of having dissembled his identity, of calling himself 'Hastings', of wearing a velvet hat and a feather, a buff leather jerkin and velvet venetians; of having 'wrought a hugger-mugger'. They read Campion's note to Pounde, quoted above, in which he denied having revealed

any 'secrets'. They produced papers found in some of the
houses where he had visited, containing a form of oath
against her Majesty. Campion replied:

> Neither is there, neither can there be anything
> imagined more directly contrary or repugnant to my
> calling than upon any occasion to administer an oath.
> But, admit I am authorized, what necessity imported
> that reason, that neither being set down in my hand-
> writing nor otherwise derived by any proof from my-
> self, but only found in places where I resorted, there-
> fore I should be he by whom they were ministered?
> This is but a naked presumption (who seeth it not?) and
> nothing vehement nor of force against me.

The two rack-masters, Norton and Hamond, gave evidence that, under torture, Campion could not be brought
to a clear answer on the Bull for the Queen's excommunication. Eliot was called; he described his visit to Lyford, and
reported that in Campion's sermon he had spoken of 'a great
day' that was shortly to come.

> QUEEN'S COUNSEL: So, what would you wish more
> manifest? The great day is threatened, comfortable to
> them and terrible to us; and what day should that be
> but that wherein the Pope, the King of Spain, and the
> Duke of Florence have appointed to invade this realm?
> CAMPION: O Judas! Judas! No other day was in my
> mind, I protest, than that wherein it should please God
> to make a restitution of faith and religion. Whereupon,
> as in every pulpit every Protestant doth, I pronounced

a great day, not wherein any temporal potentate should minister, but wherein the terrible Judge should reveal all men's consciences and try every man of each kind of religion. This is the day of change, this is the great day which I threatened.

A witness named Anthony Munday was called. He was a professional informer who had recently hung about Dr. Allen's seminary, practising as a Catholic, and seeking to gain the confidence of the *émigrés*. He published reports of Campion's capture, of the trial and of the execution; some years later he wrote a play rehabilitating Sir John Oldcastle's reputation, which, until the imposture was detected, he ascribed to Shakespeare; he attached himself to Topcliffe's staff, but got into trouble for robbing a widow of £40 under colour of searching her house for *Agnus Dei*'s. Munday testified that the English at Rheims spoke treason and that Campion had at a later time had conference with Allen; the charge to which he had already replied.

This concluded the case against Campion, for which he was to go to the gallows. Of the detailed plot to murder the Queen of which he was indicted, no evidence had been offered. Treasonable papers (whether genuine or not it is impossible to say with any certainty) had been found in some houses where he had stayed; he had dined with Allen and walked about the garden with him after dinner; he had received financial assistance for his mission from the Pope; he was a priest who had travelled about the country in lay attire. This was the case on which the Crown lawyers were demanding the death penalty.

A letter was then read—the author is not named in the report—saying that Sherwin at the fireside of the seminary had been heard to remark that one Arundel, in Cornwall, could levy a great army, and that St. Michael's Mount would be the best landing place for an invasion. Sherwin took an oath that he had never said any such thing.

It was alleged of Bosgrave that he had heard some rumours abroad of a projected invasion and, by not disclosing them, had made himself privy to treason. Campion interposed in his favour:

> ... Who findeth it not by daily experience, how that in every city, every village, and in most barber's shops, in all England, many speeches, both of estates and commonwealths, be tossed, which were never meant nor determined of in the court? If it be so in England shall we not look for the like in Italy, Flanders, France and Spain? . . . Were it not then a great point of credulity for a man divided from England with a many seas and lands, upon a matter only blazed among the vulgar people, either by journey or letter to certify the Queen's Council or commonalty of things never purposed, much less put into practice? . . . Supposing he had done as you would have had him, what had come of it? Marry, then, greater danger for slandering the realm, and how little thanks for his false information.

Cottam was accused of possessing a book named *Tractatus Conscientiae,* containing advice for making equivocal answers.

Eliot gave evidence against Johnson that he had adjured him, at Lady Petre's house, to keep secret any plots which Payne had disclosed to him. Johnson denied any such conversation.

Munday gave evidence against Rishton that he had great cunning in the manufacture of fireworks, and that he was about to burn the Queen in her barge with 'a confection of wild fire'; an enterprise which was to be followed by the general massacre of all who were ignorant of the password 'Jesus Maria'. Rishton denied all pyrotechnic knowledge.

Sledd, the informer mentioned in the preceding chapter, who had at one time been a daily communicant at Rome and Rheims, testified against Kirby, that he had come to his, Sledd's, bedside when he was ill and told him of the projected invasion, had attended a sermon of Allen's in which the priests were advised to prepare the English for the invaders, had spoken of Elizabeth as the Whore of Babylon, and expressed his intention of murdering her. Kirby denied the entire allegation.

Munday deposed against Orton that he had told him at Lyons that Elizabeth was not lawfully Queen. Orton denied ever having met Munday at Lyons or anywhere else. This concluded the evidence.

Throughout the day the Chief Justice had conducted the trial with an appearance of impartiality. The gang—Sledd, Eliot, Munday and Caddy—had sworn to the evidence for which they had been paid; the prisoners had been given the opportunity of denying it; everything had been done in order. Only once had the semblance of legality broken down, when Sherwin was comparing his work under a

hostile Government to that of the Fathers of the primitive
Church under the pagan Emperors. Then one of the justices
—Ayloff?—had forgotten his part, and, assuming the role
of prosecutor, interposed: 'But your case differeth from
theirs in the primitive Church, for those Apostles and
preachers never conspired the death of these Emperors.'

No one protested. No one hoped for anything in that
shabby pantomime. The verdict had been decided many
days before; the real judges and the real jury were in the
Council room occupied with other business.

Campion was now allowed to speak to the jury; he did
so courteously, reasonably, hopelessly:

> What charge this day you sustain, and what accompt
> you are to render at the dreadful Day of Judgement,
> whereof I could wish this also were a mirror, I trust
> there is no one of you but knoweth. I doubt not but in
> like manner you forecast how dear the innocent is to
> God, and at what price he holdeth man's blood. Here
> we are accused and impleaded to the death. We have
> no whither to appeal but to your consciences.

He showed how the most part of the evidence was general
and vague, a matter of conjecture and capricious association.
Only a few particulars had been precise and damning, and
those had emanated from the gang.

> What truth may you expect from their mouths? One
> hath confessed himself a murderer [Eliot], the other
> [Munday] a detestable atheist, a profane heathen, a
> destroyer of two men already. On your consciences,

would you believe them—they that have betrayed both
God and man, nay, that have left nothing to swear by,
neither religion nor honesty? Though you would believe them, can you? . . . I commit the rest to God, and
our convictions to your good discretions.

The jury retired. Ayloff was left alone on the bench, and,
pulling off his glove, found all his hand and signet ring
bloody, 'without any wrong, pricking or hurt'. The jury
returned with the inevitable verdict. The Lord Chief Justice
demanded whether there was any cause why he should not
pass sentence of death upon the prisoners.

It was then that Campion's voice rose in triumph. He was
no longer haggling with perjurers; he spoke now, not
merely for the handful of doomed men behind him, nor to
that sordid court, but for the whole gallant company of the
English counter-Reformation; to all his contemporaries and
all the posterity of his race:

It was not our death that ever we feared. But we knew
that we were not lords of our own lives, and therefore
for want of answer would not be guilty of our deaths.
The only thing that we have now to say is, that if our
religion do make us traitors, we are worthy to be condemned; but otherwise are, and have been, as good
subjects as ever the Queen had.

In condemning us you condemn all your own
ancestors—all the ancient priests, bishops and kings—
all that was once the glory of England, the island of
saints, and the most devoted child of the See of Peter.

For what have we taught, however you may qualify

it with the odious name of treason, that they did not uniformly teach? To be condemned with these lights—not of England only, but of the world—by their degenerate descendants, is both gladness and glory to us.

God lives; posterity will live; their judgement is not so liable to corruption as that of those who are now going to sentence us to death.

The Lord Chief Justice answered:

You must go to the place from whence you came, there to remain until ye shall be drawn through the open City of London upon hurdles to the place of execution, and there be hanged and let down alive, and your privy parts cut off, and your entrails taken out and burnt in your sight; then your heads to be cut off and your bodies divided into four parts, to be disposed of at her Majesty's pleasure. And God have mercy on your souls.

As the Lord Chief Justice's final commendation sounded, with peculiar irony, through Westminster Hall, the condemned men broke into the words of the *Te Deum* and were led back in triumph to their several prisons.

Next day the remaining seven priests were tried on Burghley's indictment and—except for Collington, who could prove that he was in Grays Inn in London when he was supposed to be at Rheims—condemned in the same way.

An alibi for Ford, similar to Collington's, was offered by a priest named Nicholson, but the judges ordered the witness to be committed to prison, where he came near to death from starvation.

Campion lay in irons for eleven days between his trial and his execution. Hitherto his family have made no appearance in the story; now a sister, of whom we know nothing, came to visit him, empowered to make him a last offer of freedom and a benefice, if he would renounce his faith. There may have been other visitors—for certain details of his life in prison, such as his statement, quoted above, that in his last racking he thought they intended to kill him, can only have reached Bombinus through the report of friends —but the only one of whom we have record is George Eliot.

'If I had thought that you would have had to suffer aught but imprisonment through my accusing of you, I would never have done it,' he said, 'however I might have lost by it.'

'If that is the case,' replied Campion, 'I beseech you, in God's name, to do penance, and confess your crime, to God's glory and your own salvation.'

But it was fear for his life rather than for his soul that had brought the informer to the Tower; ever since the journey from Lyford, when the people had called him 'Judas', he had been haunted by the spectre of Catholic reprisal.

'You are much deceived,' said Campion, 'if you think the Catholics push their detestation and wrath as far as revenge; yet to make you quite safe, I will, if you please, recommend you to a Catholic duke in Germany, where you may live in perfect security.'

But it was another man who was saved by the offer.

Eliot went back to his trade of spy; Delahays, Campion's jailer, who was present at the interview, was so moved by Campion's generosity that he became a Catholic.

London was very gay that winter. Anjou was there with his suite and the Court was wholly given over to their entertainment. Sidney, out of favour with the Queen, was engaged with the *Apologie for Poetrie.* The 'little frog' was the man of the moment, and to him various friends of Campion resorted in the hope of gaining his intercession. They found him skipping about the tennis court. It was the day before Campion's execution and, by the aid of the French abbé who acted as the Duke's confessor, they were able to obtain an interview. The little man listened to what they had to say; he looked at them stupidly, as though he were just awakened from a deep sleep, scratched his beard and then, turning on his heel, with the one word 'Play', resumed the interrupted service.

Campion's last days were occupied entirely with his preparation for death; even in the cell he was able to practise mortifications; he fasted and remained sleepless on his knees for two nights in prayer and meditation.

Sherwin and Briant had been chosen as his companions at the scaffold. They met at the Coleharbour Tower, early in the morning of 1 December, and were left together while a search was made for the clothes in which Campion had been arrested; it had been decided to execute him in the buff leather jerkin and velvet venetians which had been so ridiculed at his trial. But the garments had already been misappropriated, and he was finally led out in the gown of Irish frieze which he had worn in prison.

It was raining; it had been raining for some days, and the roads of the city were foul with mud. A great crowd had collected at the gates. 'God save you all, gentlemen,' Campion greeted them. 'God bless you, and make you good Catholics.' There were two horses, each with a hurdle at his tail. Campion was bound to one of them, Briant and Sherwin together on the other.

Then they were slowly dragged through the mud and rain, up Cheapside, past St. Martin le Grand and Newgate, along Holborn to Tyburn. Charke plodded along beside the hurdle, still eager to thrash out to the last word the question of Justification by Faith alone, but Campion seemed not to notice him; over Newgate Arch stood a figure of Our Lady which had so far survived the Anglican hammers. Campion saluted her as he passed. Here and there along the road a Catholic would push himself through the crowd and ask Campion's blessing. One witness, who supplied Bombinus with many details of this last morning, followed close at hand and stood by the scaffold. He records how one gentleman, 'either for pity or affection, most courteously wiped' Campion's 'face all spattered with mire and dirt, as he was drawn most miserably through thick and thin; for which charity or haply some sudden moved affection, God reward and bless him.'

The scene at Tyburn was tumultuous. Sir Thomas More had stepped out into the summer sunshine, to meet death quietly and politely at a single stroke of the axe. Every circumstance of Campion's execution was vile and gross.

Sir Francis Knollys, Lord Howard, Sir Henry Lee and other gentlemen of fashion were already waiting beside the scaffold. When the procession arrived, they were disputing whether the motion of the sun from east to west was violent or natural; they postponed the discussion to watch Campion, bedraggled and mudstained, mount the cart which stood below the gallows. The noose was put over his neck. The noise of the crowd was continuous, and only those in his immediate neighbourhood could hear him as he began to speak. He had it in mind to make some religious exhortation.

> *Spectaculum facti sumus Deo, angelis et hominibus* [he began]. These are the words of St. Paul, Englished thus, 'We are made a spectacle unto God, unto his angels and unto men,' verified this day in me, who am here a spectacle unto my Lord God, a spectacle unto his angels and unto you men.

But he was not allowed to continue. Sir Francis Knollys interrupted, shouting up at him to confess his treason.

> As to the treasons which have been laid to my charge [he said] and for which I am come here to suffer, I desire you all to bear witness with me that I am thereof altogether innocent.

One of the Council cried that it was too late to deny what had been proved in the court.

> Well, my Lord [he replied], I am a Catholic man and a priest; in that faith have I lived and in that faith I intend to die. If you esteem my religion treason, then am I guilty; as for other treason I never committed any, God is my judge. But you have now what you desire.

I beseech you to have patience, and suffer me to speak a word or two for discharge of my conscience.

But the gentlemen round the gallows would not let him go forward; they still heckled him about his letter to Pounde, about the invasion by the Pope and the Duke of Florence.

In a few halting sentences he made himself heard above the clamour. He forgave the jury and asked forgiveness of any whose names he might have compromised during his examination; he addressed himself to Sir Francis Knollys on Richardson's behalf, saying that, to his knowledge, that man had never in his possession a copy of the book which the informers declared they had found in his baggage.

Then a schoolmaster named Hearne stood forward and read a proclamation in the Queen's name, that the execution they were to witness that morning was for treason and not for religion. Campion stood in prayer. The Lords of the Council still shouted up questions to him about the Bull of Excommunication, but now Campion would not answer and stood with his head bowed and his hands folded on his breast. An Anglican clergyman attempted to direct his prayers, but he answered gently, 'Sir, you and I are not one in religion, wherefore I pray you content yourself. I bar none of prayer; but I only desire them that are of the household of faith to pray with me, and in mine agony to say one creed.'

They called to him to pray in English, but he replied with great mildness that 'he would pray God in a language which they both well understood'.

There was more noise; the Councillors demanded that he should ask the Queen's forgiveness.

'Wherein have I offended her? In this I am innocent. This is my last speech; in this give me credit—I have and do pray for her.'

Still the courtiers were not satisfied. Lord Howard demanded to know what queen he prayed for.

'Yea, for Elizabeth your Queen and my Queen, unto whom I wish a long quiet reign with all prosperity.'

The cart was then driven from under him, the eager crowd swayed forward, and Campion was left hanging, until, unconscious, perhaps already dead, he was cut down and the butcher began his work.

When the spectacle was over the crowd dispersed. An emotional witness records that several thousand were turned to the Faith by the events of that day. Many thousands there have been, but they were not in that assembly. The Elizabethan mob dearly loved a bloody execution, and any felon was the hero of a few hours, whatever his crimes. If any felt uneasy about the Queen's justice, there were gentler pleasures to attract their minds; in particular two Dutchmen, who were the rage of the moment; the one was seven feet seven inches in height, 'comelie of person but lame of the legs (for he had broken them of lifting a barrel of beer)'; his companion was a midget who could walk between the giant's legs, wearing a feather in his cap; he had 'never a good foot nor any knee at all and yet could dance a gallard, no arm but a stump on which he could dance a cup and after toss it about three or four times and every time receive the same on the said stump'. With distractions of this kind the fate of the three priests was soon forgotten. One man, however, returned from Tyburn to Grays Inn profoundly changed; Henry Walpole, Cambridge wit, minor poet, satirist, flaneur, a young man of birth, popular, intelligent, slightly romantic. He came of a Catholic family and occasionally expressed Catholic sentiments, but until that day had kept at a discreet distance from Gilbert and his circle, and was on good terms with authority. He was a typical member of that easy-going majority, on whom the success of the Elizabethan Settlement depended, who would have preferred to live under a Catholic régime but accepted the change without very serious regret. He had an interest in theology and had attended Campion's conferences with the Anglican clergy. He secured a front place at Tyburn; so close that when Campion's entrails were torn out by the butcher and thrown into the cauldron of boiling water, a spot of blood splashed upon his coat. In that moment he was caught into a new life; he crossed the sea, became a priest, and, thirteen years later, after very terrible sufferings, died the same death as Campion's on the gallows at York.

And so the work of Campion continued; so it continues. He was one of a host of martyrs, each, in their several ways, gallant and venerable; some performed more sensational feats of adventure, some sacrificed more conspicuous positions in the world, many suffered crueller tortures, but to his own, and to each succeeding generation, Campion's fame has burned with unique warmth and brilliance; it was his genius to express, in sentences that have resounded across the centuries, the spirit of chivalry in which they suffered, to typify in his zeal, his innocence, his inflexible purpose, the pattern which they followed.

Years later, in the sombre, sceptical atmosphere of the eighteenth century, Bishop Challoner set himself to sift out and collect the English martyrology. The Catholic cause was very near to extinction in England. Families who had resisted the onset of persecution were quietly conforming under neglect. The Church survived here and there in scattered households, regarded by the world as, at the best, something Gothic and slightly absurd, like a ghost or a family curse. Emancipation still lay in the distant future; no career was open to the Catholics; their only ambition was to live quietly in their houses, send their children to school abroad, pay the double land taxes, and, as best they could, avoid antagonizing their neighbours. It was then, when the whole gallant sacrifice appeared to have been prodigal and vain, that the story of the martyrs lent them strength.

We are the heirs of their conquest, and enjoy, at our ease, the plenty which they died to win.

Today a chapel stands by the site of Tyburn; in Oxford, the city he loved best, a noble college has risen dedicated in Campion's honour.

> There will never want in England men that will have care of their own salvation, nor such as shall advance other men's; neither shall this Church here ever fail so long as priests and pastors shall be found for their sheep, rage man or devil never so much.

THE END

Mells—Belton—Newton Ferrers
  October 1934—May 1935

APPENDIX

CAMPION'S BRAG

[TO THE RIGHT HONOURABLE, THE LORDS OF HER MAJESTIE'S PRIVY COUNCIL]

RIGHT HONOURABLE:

Whereas I have come out of Germanie and Boëmeland, being sent by my Superiours, and adventured myself into this noble Realm, my deare Countrie, for the glorie of God and benefit of souls, I thought it like enough that, in this busie, watchful and suspicious worlde, I should either sooner or later be intercepted and stopped of my course. Wherefore, providing for all events, and uncertaine what may become of me, when God shall haply deliver my body into durance, I supposed it needful to put this writing in a readiness, desiringe your good Lordships to give it y^r reading, for to know my cause. This doing, I trust I shall ease you of some labour. For that which otherwise you must have sought for by practice of wit, I do now lay into your hands by plaine confession. And to ye intent that the whole matter may be conceived in order, and so the better both understood and remembered, I make thereof these ix points or articles, directly, truly and resolutely opening my full enterprise and purpose.

i. I confess that I am (albeit unworthie) a priest of ye Catholike Church, and through ye great mercie of God vowed now these viii years into the Religion of the Societie of Jhesus. Hereby I have taken upon me a special kind of warfare under the banner of obedience, and eke resigned all my interest or possibilitie of wealth, honour, pleasure and other worldlie felicitie.

ii. At the voice of our General Provost, which is to me a warrant from heaven, and Oracle of Christ, I tooke my voyage from Prage to Rome (where our said General Father is always resident) and from Rome to England, as I might and would have done joyously into any part of Christendome or Heathenesse, had I been thereto assigned.

iii. My charge is, of free cost to preach the Gospel, to minister the Sacraments, to instruct the simple, to reforme sinners, to confute errors—in brief, to crie alarme spiritual against foul vice and proud ignorance, wherewith many my dear Countrymen are abused.

iv. I never had mind, and am strictly forbidden by our Father that sent me, to deal in any respect with matter of State or Policy of this realm, as things which appertain not to my vocation, and from which I do gladly restrain and sequester my thoughts.

v. I do ask, to the glory of God, with all humility, and under your correction, iii sortes of indifferent and quiet audiences: *the first* before your Honours, wherein I will discourse of religion, so far as it toucheth the common weale and your nobilities: *the second,* whereof I make more account, before the Doctors and Masters and chosen men of both Universities, wherein I undertake to avow the faith of our Catholike Church by proofs innumerable, Scriptures, Councils, Fathers, History, natural and moral reasons: *the third* before the lawyers, spiritual and temporal, wherein I will justify the said faith by the common wisdom of the laws standing yet in force and practice.

vi. I would be loth to speak anything that might sound of any insolent brag or challenge, especially being now as a dead man to this world and willing to put my head under every man's foot, and to kiss the ground they tread upon. Yet have I such a courage in avouching the Majesty of Jhesus my King, and such affiance in his gracious favour, and such assurance in my quarrel, and my evidence so impregnable, and because I know perfectly that no one Protestant, nor all the Protestants living, nor any sect of our adversaries (however they face men down in pulpits, and overrule us in their kingdom of grammarians and unlearned ears) can maintain their doctrine in disputation. I am to sue most humbly and instantly for the combat with all and every of them, and the most principal that may be found: protesting that in this trial the better furnished they come, the better welcome they shall be.

vii. And because it hath pleased God to enrich the Queen my Sovereign Ladye with notable gifts of nature, learning, and princely education, I do verily trust that—if her Highness would vouchsafe her royal person and good attention to such a conference as, in the ii part of my fifth article I have motioned, or to a few sermons, which in her or your hearing I am to utter,—such manifest and fair light by good method and plain dealing may be cast upon these controversies, that possibly her zeal of truth and love of her people shall incline her noble Grace to disfavour some proceedings hurtful to the Realm, and procure towards us oppressed more equitie.

viii. Moreover I doubt not but you her Highness' Council being of such wisdom and discreet in cases most important, when you shall have heard these questions of religion opened faithfully, which many times by our adversaries are huddled up and confounded, will see upon what substantial grounds our Catholike Faith is builded, how feeble that side is which by sway of the time prevaileth against us, and so at last for your own souls, and for many thousand souls that depend upon your government, will discountenance error when it is bewrayed, and hearken to those who would spend the best blood in their bodies for your salvation. Many innocent hands are lifted up to heaven for you daily by those English students, whose posteritie shall never die, which beyond seas, gathering virtue and sufficient knowledge for the purpose, are determined never to give you over, but either to win you heaven, or to die upon your pikes. And touching our Societie, be it known to you that we have made a league —all the Jesuits in the world, whose succession and multitude must overreach all the practices of England—cheerfully to carry the cross you shall lay upon us, and never to despair your recovery, while we have a man left to enjoy your Tyburn, or to be racked with your torments, or consumed with your prisons. The expense is reckoned, the enterprise is begun; it is of God, it cannot be withstood. So the faith was planted: so it must be restored.

ix. If these my offers be refused, and my endeavours can take no place, and I, having run thousands of miles to do you good, shall be rewarded with rigour, I have no more to say but to recommend your case and mine to Almightie God, the Searcher of Hearts, who send us His grace, and set us at accord before the day of payment, to the end we may at last be friends in heaven, when all injuries shall be forgotten.

Other Paperbacks from Oxford

★

SELECTIONS FROM CLARENDON

With a new foreword by HUGH TREVOR-ROPER

Clarendon's writings have always given pleasure to admirers of a full, flowing, and vigorous style. They remain an important source for historians of the period 1640–67; but they have a quite separate value in the vivid gallery of portraits and the epigrammatic judgements on men and events that the author provides. In particular, Clarendon's *History of the Rebellion* is acknowledged as a classic of historical writing and of political philosophy which anticipates the work of Hume, Burke, and Acton. This is a reissue in a larger format of the selection first published in the World's Classics series in 1955, from the *History of the Rebellion* and Clarendon's autobiography, *The Life by Himself.*

THE CONCISE OXFORD DICTIONARY OF THE CHRISTIAN CHURCH

Edited by E. A. LIVINGSTONE

This abridged version of the second edition of *The Oxford Dictionary of the Christian Church* makes available for the more general reader, in a quarter of the length of the parent volume, the vast majority of the entries in that unique reference book. The range of the *Concise Dictionary* is considerable. It covers the major Christian feasts and denominations and includes accounts of the lives of the saints, résumés of Patristic writings, histories of heretical sects, and outlines of the opinions of major theologians and moral philosophers. Many related subjects are also explored in this comprehensive work: there are entries on painters, sculptors, and composers; non-Christian religions and rituals; famous cathedrals; and significant discoveries in textual criticism and archaeology.

THE REFORMATION IN ENGLAND

Maurice Powicke

'Within his self-imposed limitations, the work could not have been more brilliantly done.' *Times Literary Supplement*

'The one definite thing which can be said about the Reformation in England is that it was an act of State.' Sir Maurice Powicke sets out to give a dispassionate account of the actual process of the Reformation, without passing any judgement on the profound theological and moral issues involved.

His study is an attempt to explain the way in which the transition from the medieval system to the organization of the Church in Tudor times was effected and the changes which this transition involved. It was by these political moves and these social adjustments more than any others that the English State and people were transformed from their medieval to their modern character.

The book has long been prized for its clear analysis of a vexed period and the intuitive sympathy with which Sir Maurice regarded men as diverse as Sir Thomas More, Archbishop Cranmer, Bishop Gardiner, and Cardinal Pole.

THE EARLY CHRISTIAN FATHERS

Edited and Translated by HENRY BETTENSON

'the extracts are sufficiently numerous and full to give the authentic flavour of Tertullian or Origen or Irenaeus or Cyprian. Notes are provided where needed, and the introductions are full and up to date.' *The Guardian*

There is now a wide and growing appreciation of the value and relevance of the writings of the Fathers of the early Church, even for non-academic readers, and particularly for all who wish to understand Christian doctrine. The authors represented in this volume, first published in 1956, are the principal writers of the Church in the Roman Empire from the period immediately after the New Testament down to the age of Constantine and the Council of Nicaea (A.D. 325). They include St. Ignatius of Antioch, St. Justin, Tertullian, St. Irenaeus, St. Clement of Alexandria, Origen, St. Cyprian, and St. Athanasius. Mr. Bettenson has selected passages to display as fully as possible the thought of the early Fathers, especially on the great doctrinal themes, and has himself translated them afresh, with brief annotation where necessary.

THE LATER CHRISTIAN FATHERS

Edited and Translated by HENRY BETTENSON

The century and a quarter following the Council of Nicaea has been called the 'Golden Age of Patristic literature'. It is this period that Henry Bettenson covers in this companion volume to *The Early Christian Fathers*, selecting from the writings of Basil the Great, Gregory of Nyssa, Jerome, Augustine of Hippo, Cyril of Alexandria, and other Fathers of the Christian Church. Their central concerns were formulating the doctrine of the Trinity after the Nicene conclusions, and enunciating the doctrine of the divinity and humanity of Christ. The writings served to clarify if not to solve the issues and they continue to be valuable and relevant for all who wish to understand the Christian doctrine. As in *The Early Christian Fathers*, Mr. Bettenson has translated everything afresh and provided some annotation and brief sketches of the lives of each of the Fathers represented in the selection.

DOCUMENTS OF THE CHRISTIAN CHURCH

Selected and Edited by HENRY BETTENSON

First published in 1943, this book won a world-wide reputation, so that 'Bettenson, *Documents*' is now referred to as a sourcebook in many important works. It is also fascinating reading, containing 'the hard facts of many disputed questions, the ammunition for controversy, the corrective to loose thinking and idle speech'. In 1963 it went into a second edition, so that it now covers an additional twenty years of Christian history, from the earliest documents after the New Testament, down to the eve of the Second Vatican Council. It spans the periods of the Fathers and the Middle Ages, Roman Catholic and Protestant churches, the Reformation, the Churches in Great Britain, and the beginning of the Ecumenical Movement, giving an indispensable background to history and current events.

'That invaluable Christian reference book' *Church Times*

'Covering the whole range of Christian history, it is specially valuable to the young Student.' *Church Quarterly Review*

'This source book can be used to make your own Do-it-yourself Church History. Here is varied material about which you can make up your own mind, with no partisan scholar coming in between.' *Methodist Magazine*

ENGLISH TOWNS IN TRANSITION 1500–1700

PETER CLARK AND PAUL SLACK

Between 1500 and 1700 there was a major transition in the development of English towns. With the Reformation, many of the traditional features of towns were destroyed, and it was not until 1700 that a new urban stability was beginning to emerge from the political and economic crises of the later sixteenth and the seventeenth century.

In their early chapters Peter Clark and Paul Slack look in turn at the different kinds of town, including the county towns and new industrial centres, and describe their salient aspects. In the second half of the book they adopt a thematic rather than a chronological approach: they explore the changes which affected all towns—and the pressures which afflicted them—by examining their demographic and social structures, their economic and political functions, and their cultural influence. The result is a lucid synthesis of recent research in urban and local history; and in reconstructing a picture of the quality of life in Tudor and Stuart towns, the authors also present an analysis of the historical processes which decisively shaped early modern urban society.

'a compact, up-to-date, and stimulating synthesis' *Times Higher Education Supplement*

'most welcome. The authors have produced a lucid, readable and learned survey, admirably organised and based on all the recent work.' *Yorkshire Post*

'For students seeking an introduction to urban history, this is the place to begin.' *History*

THE ECONOMY OF ENGLAND 1450-1750

D. C. COLEMAN

Two centuries ago the Industrial Revolution began transforming the economy of England into the form in which we know it today. But what sort of economy did England have in preceding centuries? Professor Coleman gives us an account of three centuries of English economic life, stretching from the Wars of the Roses almost to the accession of George III. He never allows us to forget that the economic world in which the men and women of the day lived and died was only one aspect of their historical context. And just as he puts the economy of England into its social and political setting, so he also presents it in its changing relationship with the economy of Europe and the wider world. In this last connection the period from 1650 to 1750, rarely treated as a whole, receives particular emphasis as marking the economic divergence of England from the Continent.

'Professor Coleman brings a welcome freshness of learning and originality of style to the subject-matter which makes this work an excellent statement of the more temperate position which lies between "old" and "new" economic historians.' Barry Supple, *Times Literary Supplement*